THE UNIVERSITY OF MICHIGAN
CENTER FOR CHINESE STUDIES

MICHIGAN PAPERS IN CHINESE STUDIES
NO. 33

CENTRAL DOCUMENTS AND POLITBURO POLITICS IN CHINA

by

Kenneth Lieberthal
with the assistance of
James Tong and Sai-cheung Yeung

Ann Arbor

Center for Chinese Studies
The University of Michigan

1978

Open access edition funded by the National Endowment for the Humanities/ Andrew W. Mellon Foundation Humanities Open Book Program.

Library of Congress Cataloging in Publication Data

Lieberthal, Kenneth.
Central documents and Politburo politics in China.

(Michigan papers in Chinese studies; no. 33)
Includes bibliographical references.
1. China--Politics and government--1949-1976.
2. China--Politics and government--1976-
3. Chung-kuo kung ch'an tang. Chung yang wei yüen hui.
4. Chung-kuo kung ch'an tang. Chung yang cheng chih chü. 5. China--Government publications. I. Tong, James, 1947- joint author. II. Yeung, Sai-cheung, joint author. III. Title. IV. Series.

JQ1509 1978. L53 354'.51 78-8740
ISBN 0-89264-033-2

Printed and bound by CPI Group (UK) Ltd, Croydon, CR0 4YY

ISBN 978-0-89264-033-1 (paper)
ISBN 978-0-472-12754-2 (ebook)
ISBN 978-0-472-90149-4 (open access)

To my parents

Milton and Naomi Lieberthal

CONTENTS

ACKNOWLEDGMENTS

I undertook the research for this study at the Center for Chinese Studies of the University of Michigan and benefited greatly from the excellent working facilities and staff support provided by the Center. James Tong and Sai-cheung Yeung made major contributions to this project, each in his own way having far more input than is usually conveyed by the rubric "research assistant." I owe a deep debt of gratitude to each. Sophia Lee put together the information in Appendix II from my scattered files, typed the initial draft of the manuscript, made important editorial suggestions, and assisted in certain phases of the research. Her dedication and good judgment have thus played a significant role in bring this project to fruition. Marlene Thom worked with great speed and skill in improving the quality of the presentation and husbanding the manuscript through the editorial and publication processes.

I have also benefited from the comments of a number of my colleagues. Most of these were made in response to presentations of portions of this study in seminars at the University of Michigan, Harvard University, Columbia University, George Washington University, and the Department of State. Michel Oksenberg and Gregory Shaw read the entire manuscript and made important and useful suggestions.

The research for this study was supported by the Department of State under Contract No. 1722-620042. Views and conclusions contained in this study do not represent the official opinion or policy of the Department of State.

I am very grateful to M. E. Sharpe, Publisher, for permission to use the translation of the "Outline Summary Report of the Work of the Academy of Sciences" contained in Appendix I. This translation also appears in <u>Chinese Law and Government</u>, vol. XI.

Neither the organizations nor the individuals mentioned above are responsible for the views, interpretations and misinterpretations that appear on the following pages. All errors of fact and judgment are my own, but they would have been more numerous by far had it not been for those whose generous assistance is acknowledged here.

INTRODUCTION

Virtually every analysis of Chinese politics views the Politburo as the nerve center of the system, but questions abound as to how this center governs itself and how it interacts with the system around it. Specifically, how much consultation occurs during the drafting of major Politburo documents, and who is brought into this process? How is information channeled up to this body, and what are the rules that govern the access of the Politburo members themselves to data generated by the bureaucracies? How are the political strategies of individual leaders and political factions attuned to this system of information channeling? What types of decisions are reached by the Politburo? To whom are they communicated? How rigidly must they be followed? How institutionalized is this entire decision making system, and has it become more--or less--institutionalized over the years? How has the factional legacy of the Cultural Revolution affected its mode of operations? Indeed, in the wake of the Cultural Revolution, how much in control of the system has the Politburo itself been?

Scholars to date have looked at the apex of the Chinese polity from a range of angles--by analyzing factional conflict among the leaders,[1] through studying the evolution of programs in a particular issue area,[2] by dividing the system into various policy arenas,[3] and via focusing on the process of consultation among the leaders.[4] This study takes a rather different approach to the task. It seeks to understand better the questions raised above by analyzing a particular stream of largely intra-bureaucratic communications in the Chinese system: the so-called "Central Documents" (CDs).[5] This is the series of documents through which the top Party leadership directly communicates with the rest of the political system. While officially regarded as "Central Committee" documents, the overwhelming majority of these have in fact been adopted by a smaller group--the Politburo, its Standing Committee, or even by Mao Tse-tung alone in the name of the Central Committee. Some have been adopted at large meetings that bring together a considerable range of Party leaders, as detailed below, and a very few have actually issued from Central Committee plenums and been published in the media at the conclusion of these gatherings. This last group clearly differs from the larger class of Central Documents of which it is a part, however, and is therefore omitted from consideration in this study.

The political environment within which the Central Document system is nested is one marked by a constant tension between formal organizations and procedures, recognized as indispensable for governing a vast country, and informal means of deliberating and communicating, required to circumvent bureaucratic rigidities while maintaining strict secrecy. Although study of the Central Document system of necessity focuses more on the formal dimensions of the policy process at the highest levels, political strategies inevitably intrude and affect such fundamental choices as whether or not to use the Central Document system in the first place. The top Party leaders, after all, enjoy a wide variety of options for communicating information to lower levels.

Structurally, the Central Document series is only one of an impressive array of document streams that flow from Peking to the lower levels of the political hierarchy. Each major Central organ, for example, can issue its own documents, and almost certainly the Politburo can channel information into any of these other document series (such as that of the State Council or the Military Commission, as appropriate). Indeed, given the fact that most members of the Politburo simultaneously hold at least one major post in another leading organ,[6] it is possible that key individuals might use their special access to these other document streams to convey information that they do not want funneled through the Politburo itself.

Changing relationships among China's major bureaucracies--the Party, PLA and government--also may have contoured the use of the CD network at different periods. In brief, the government apparatus under Chou En-lai maximized its role during the First Five Year Plan of 1953-57, the Party hierarchy under Liu Shao-ch'i largely ran the Great Leap Forward in 1958-62, and the PLA under Lin Piao picked up the pieces from the shambles of the Cultural Revolution in the late 1960s. In all likelihood, as Chou, Liu and Lin successively assumed the key roles under Mao in the system, they shunted an increasing range of issues into the document stream of their own bureaucracy.[7] Only for Liu would this be the Central Document system. There is some evidence that this changing set of relationships among China's three major bureaucracies did indeed affect the use of the Central Document series,[8] although too little information is available to draw firm conclusions on this issue.

The Central Document series was shaped also by the fact that Mao Tse-tung clearly tried to "capture" this document stream and make it "his" vehicle for intrabureaucratic communications. As noted below, Mao in 1953 declared that he personally had to peruse all Central Documents before they were issued in order for them to be considered valid. He seems, moreover, on occasion to have had CDs issued on his own authority. While Mao demonstrably did not limit himself to Central Documents in communicating with lower levels of the political hierarchy,[9] his sitting astride this particular document stream meant, concretely, that no documents could be issued in the name of the Central Committee that had not received his personal assent.

This situation, as explained below, created a special incentive for other leaders to attempt to manipulate the Central Document series to support their views on issues of concern. Alternatively, these leaders could resort to the other document streams to which they had legitimate access by virtue of concomitant positions they held. Some, such as the so-called "Gang of Four," also used their own informal document distribution system based on personal ties. The Gang's network diverged sharply from the Central Document system and was used for issues on which the radicals could not obtain the backing of Mao and the rest of the Politburo.[10]

Thus, the use of CDs must be seen as a political decision, affected but not wholly determined by bureaucratic rules and regulations that govern the flow of documents in China. Within this context, the following analysis approaches the Central Document system via four basic sets of questions: first, what are "Central Documents," i.e., how are they differentiated from the numerous other document series that carry communications from Peking to the provinces; why are some issues slated for inclusion in CDs and others not; and, substantively, what types of communications do CDs carry from the Party Center? Second, how are Central Documents drafted and adopted? Third, to whom are their contents transmitted, and how is this done? And fourth, what does an analysis of this bureaucratic instrument of communications tell us about the range of questions concerning the Chinese political system raised above?

When dealing with a subject such as Central Documents, problems of evidence warrant special mention. A large number of these documents have become available in the West through various channels over the years,[11] but in many cases it is impossible to establish their authenticity and accuracy. The Chinese government has chosen to release the texts of only very few of these documents.[12] Even where documents are available, moreover, data on such crucial issues as the rules that govern access to information among members of the Politburo and the handling of different types of Central Documents as they are transmitted down the hierarchy are spotty, at best. Thus, the lacunae are numerous and difficult to fill with confidence.

In this regard, the following study benefited greatly from interviews conducted with several former cadres in the PRC. Since none of these informants had themselves participated in the drafting or adoption of any Central Documents, however, their information was of indirect assistance, at best. Essentially, through explaining how documents were handled at other levels of the political hierarchy, they provided the basis for formulating a set of ideas about Central level decision making and document flows that could be tested against the available data concerning CDs. This proved invaluable in developing a conceptual framework within which to view the Central Documents, often highlighting information in the available documents and the Chinese media that I otherwise might have glossed over. Thus, my intellectual debt to these interviewees is great, and I regret that I must respect their wishes and thank them anonymously for their important contributions. At the same time, since none of these informants had direct knowledge of the drafting and adoption processes of Central Documents, the core of this study rests solely on analysis of the documentary sources available, as cited in the footnotes.

The grey areas that remain after an analysis of the available evidence pertaining to the Central Document system are uncomfortably large. This study attempts to sketch in these areas, occasionally on the basis of evidence that is more suggestive than definitive. The operative assumption that guides this presentation is that it is important to specify as clearly and fully as possible the characteristics of the Chinese Central Document system as these are revealed by currently available evidence. The resulting explicit and detailed picture can be tested and refined by future data as they become available.

A brief note on the Appendices. Chapter II analyzes the process by which two of the most important documents of the 1970s, "Some Questions on Accelerating the Development of Industry" and the "Outline Summary Report of the Work of the Academy of Sciences," were defined. Appendix I provides translations of the latest available texts of these documents. Both were drafted during 1975 and became operational (possibly in slightly modified form) in the late spring of 1977. They give an extraordinarily detailed explication of the basic policy in the economy and in science and technology during 1977-78. Appendix II lists all known Central Documents issued during 1966-77 and supplies relevant bibliographic data so as to facilitate further research on the Central Document system in China.

I. THE CENTRAL DOCUMENT SERIES

Document Series in the People's Republic of China

The Central Document series, as noted above, is only one of a number of streams of documents that flow from Central to local authorities in China. The documents in each of these series are numbered *seriatim* starting with the number 1 each calendar year. They are also labeled with a *pien-hao* that indicates the institution that issues them. *Chung-fa* is the Chinese label currently used for Central Documents. Thus, for example, the twelfth Central Document issued in 1977 would be labeled "*Chung-fa* (77) #12," with the number in parentheses indicating the year of issue.

The State Council's own document series tends to concentrate on issues that are narrowly technical or specialized in nature. This State Council series typically is far longer than its Central Committee counterpart, probably because the former plays a more central role in day-to-day operations of the government and economy. Each ministry, State Council commission and committee, and Central Committee department (including the General Office of the Central Committee) also has its own document series.[13]

Regulations governing the circulation of official documents, as well as political considerations, influence which document series will be used to handle a particular issue.[14] The basic rule is that a superior unit may communicate in a downward direction only with subordinate units that duplicate its position in the system at each level of the hierarchy. Laterally, a specialized unit at any level can communicate directly with the Party or state committee at that level and vice versa. A specialized Party unit can also communicate with its government counterpart at the same level. Thus, for example, the Ministry of Education can send documents to--and receive them from--education departments under the revolutionary committees at the province, *hsien*, or other levels. The Education Ministry can also participate in a two-way document flow with the State Council. Should the Education Ministry leadership want to send a document to the Revolutionary Committee of Liaoning Province, however, it would not be allowed to do so. Rather, it would have to request the State Council to send out the appropriate document, as the Council alone can communicate directly with the committees at each level. The same principle holds true in both the Party and state hierarchies and clearly produces bureaucratic rationales to direct certain types of information through a particular document series instead of via another channel of communication. A provincial Party committee, for instance, can receive formal, direct written instructions from Peking only via the Central Document stream.[15] The rigidities of this system are partially mitigated through the ability of the initiating organ to specify other units that should receive copies of a document strictly for reference (ch'ao-sung chi-kuan), although limitations even on these are specified in the rules for the drafting and circulation of documents.

There are, then, many channels in the formal communications system through which information can flow between upper and lower levels in China. Most of these carry only data pertinent to a single functionally defined network in the bureaucracy, although some--such as the Central Committee Documents--can be used to communicate with a far broader range of units. Indeed, the limited data available on the CD stream provides impressive evidence of the versatility of this document series and its use in the PRC.

The Forms and Functions of Central Documents

There is a great deal of flexibility built into the Central Document system in the PRC. These documents are used to serve a range of functions--from communicating authoritative decisions to stoking up a policy discussion to circulating reference materials to citing positive and negative models for approbation or criticism. Substantively, they range across virtually all issue areas and vary from highly concrete and time-specific to broad and fundamental. They employ a range of rubrics that indicate to receiving organs how to treat the contents of the document, and most of those issued use labels that suggest that they should be followed in spirit rather than to the letter by local organs. Indeed, perhaps a majority of these documents do not even convey "decisions" in any narrow sense of the term but rather are used to circulate reference materials and perform other functions. Central

Documents also vary in their levels of classification, from some whose contents should be made widely known to the public to others that are issued only in individually numbered copies that must be secreted back to the Central Committee via special courier by a certain date. Even their role in the system vis-à-vis the other streams of communications mentioned above has changed considerably over the years.

CDs to Convey Decisions. Central Documents have been used to convey "Central Committee" decisions across the full range of issue areas--from political issues to administrative and organizational problems to economic concerns. In the political sphere, for example, the Cultural Revolution generated numerous CDs that defined the policies for carrying out this massive political campaign among various sectors of the population. Those available for late 1966 stipulated how to implement the Great Proletarian Cultural Revolution (GPCR) with respect to the rural areas,[16] urban students and teachers,[17] and workers in factories and mines,[18] among others. Each laid down a set of regulations that guided the participation of the group concerned in the movement as it mushroomed during these months. The CDs in these instances, then, provided a major tool used by the Central leadership to shape the contours of a political campaign as the movement swept across China.

In the organizational realm, the "Regulations on the Work in Rural People's Communes (Revised Draft)," which was passed in September 1962,[19] legislated the guidelines for people's communes in the aftermath of the Great Leap Forward. This document amounts to an organizational charter for communes, dealing in its various sections with the form, organization and regulations of people's communes in the current period; the administration of the commune as a whole; the production brigades; the production teams; family sideline occupations; commune members and their rights; cadres; control organizations at all levels of the commune; and the Party organization in the commune. The stipulations in this CD have provided the framework for the CCP's policies toward people's communes over the past fifteen years, and this document was clearly the vehicle for resolving a number of fundamental organizational and administrative questions about the communes that had been plaguing the Central authorities for some time.[20]

Decisions on the economy conveyed in CDs have varied immensely in scope. Some Central Documents, such as the 1961 "Seventy Articles on Industrial Policy," stipulated the basic approach to be adopted toward a major segment of the economy that would be applicable for the indefinite future.[21] Other CDs, however, have focused on a particular economic problem of limited scope and duration, as illustrated by the 1 March 1960 "Directive of the CCP Central Committee and the State Council on Fishing during the Spring High-Water Period."[22] As suggested by this example, many of these more narrowly focused directives on the economy have been issued under the joint imprimatur of the Central Committee and the State Council.

Often, Central Documents are employed to give substantively narrow decisions broader exposure. The winter 1976-77 Central Document on the situation in Yunnan Province[23] is a typical example. The Central Document format in this case made the particular measures recommended for Yunnan available for study and discussion by leading cadres throughout the country. Occasionally, as was often the case during the Cultural Revolution, the CD specifies the dimensions of the "narrow" decision to which people of other areas should pay particular attention.[24]

In a somewhat different variant, the Central Committee will often circulate a document submitted to it by a given unit or locale along with an accompanying comment. This comment not infrequently touches on one or more of the key issues raised in the document submitted and provides more widely applicable guidance on these issues.[25] At other times, the Center may simply indicate that the document submitted to it is well taken and should be implemented in a specified range of units. On 5 October 1966, for instance, the Central authorities circulated a directive of the Military Affairs Committee and the General Political Department on the Cultural Revolution in PLA academies and military schools. The CD in this case indicated simply that the Central Committee felt that this military directive is correct "and is applicable to all universities and middle schools above the county level throughout the country."[26]

Finally, many CDs focus on a particular item that appears to fall within the jurisdiction of one functional system but the proper implementation of which in fact requires the attention of appropriate Party committees at various levels. This situation virtually demands that the issue be handled by a Central Document. As previously noted, the leading organ of a given functional system, such as the Rural Work Department of the Central Committee,[27] is not permitted to communicate directly with lower level Party committees. Rather, it is restricted to direct communications only with the functional departments at each level concerned with, in this instance, rural work. Thus, should a directive on the summer harvest require appropriate assistance by the

Party committees in the rural areas, it will be sent out by the Central Committee as a CD rather than by the Rural Work Department as a document internal to that system. In this case, the use of a CD format does not indicate so much that the Central Committee or Politburo per se has seriously considered the issue or reached a formal decision on it as that the CD is providing a bureaucratic vehicle for giving a document a rational sphere of circulation in view of the efforts that will be required to carry out the tasks specified in it.

In sum, Central Documents have been used to convey the full range of decisions one would expect to emanate from the nerve center of the Chinese political system. Somewhat surprisingly, however, many CDs do not communicate "decisions" in any narrow sense of the term, as explained below.

CDs to Circulate Materials for Reference. A large number of CDs over the years have served simply as vehicles for providing documentary materials to officials at lower levels. Typically, the Central Document itself in this case consists of instructions on how to handle the materials concerned, stipulating what attitude one should adopt, to whom the materials should be communicated (if anyone), and how they should be transmitted. When the issue is one of major political interest that has still not been brought to a full conclusion by the Central authorities, these documents are evidently circulated to enable lower ranking cadres to squelch rumors and cope with difficult questions from their own subordinates and the masses. The Lin Piao affair has provided one of the most dramatic examples of this use of CDs.

Lin Piao is alleged to have perished while trying to flee by plane to the Soviet Union after an unsuccessful assassination attempt against Mao Tse-tung on 12 September 1971. On 18 September, the Central Committee issued a brief explanation of what had occurred in the form of CD (71)#60.[28] This explanation ran about 325 words in length and clearly served only as the initial communication to provide preliminary guidance to lower ranking cadres on a problem of extreme sensitivity.

The Central Committee followed this up with a series of CDs over the next year that provided lower level leaders both with materials generated by the continuing investigation of the Lin Piao affair and with guidance on how to analyze these materials and communicate them to a wider audience. CD (72)#3 stipulated the scope of circulation for these materials and appended the first batch;[29] CD (72)#4 supplied a second major batch;[30] CD (72)#12 circulated the official summary of

Mao Tse-tung's comments on his inspection tour during late summer of 1971--just prior to the Lin affair and highly pertinent to its dynamics;[31] CD (72) #24 provided the third major batch of materials generated by the Lin Piao affair investigation;[32] and CD (72) #25 communicated five documents concerning Lin Piao's works and speeches with appropriate criticisms.[33] The last of these CDs that is publicly available circulated in China fully ten months before the Central Committee Ad Hoc Team, set up to deal with this incident, had completed its investigation and presented its report. The report itself was submitted to the Central Committee for approval on 10 July 1973. It received this approval on 20 August and was then circulated as CD (73) #34 on 8 September.[34]

More recently, the rehabilitation of Teng Hsiao-p'ing and the purge of the Gang of Four occasioned similar use of the CD communications channel. At least four Central Documents attended the former process,[35] one of which conveyed the texts of two letters that Teng Hsiao-p'ing had written to Hua Kuo-feng on 10 October 1976 and 10 April 1977 respectively.[36] While these documents were being issued, moreover, the Party Center also issued a CD containing instructions concerning the nettlesome problem of political rumors.[37] In early December 1976 and then again in March 1977 the Party leadership utilized CDs to circulate extensive "reference materials" on the intrigues of the Gang of Four that had been generated during the course of the investigation of the activities of this group.[38]

In form, this type of Central Document typically carries the rubric of a "circular" (t'ung-chih) and, as mentioned above, includes the documentary materials as a series of appendices to the CD itself. In some instances, then, the Politburo uses Central Documents to provide lower levels with sensitive materials and to instruct them on how to handle these materials. The Central Documents themselves (as opposed to the materials appended to them) may run for only one or two paragraphs in length or may be as long as several pages.

Rubrics and the Handling of Central Documents. The above comments make clear that not all recipients of a CD are expected to follow to the letter the instructions contained in it. Indeed, often these documents merely provide materials that have been submitted to the Central authorities and obviously cannot be applied very rigidly in the locale to which the CD has been transmitted. How do local recipients, therefore, know how to handle the contents of a CD that has just been transmitted to them? In part, pertinent instructions may be contained in the document itself or may be communicated via briefings on the document, as described in the section on the transmission process below. Another clue, however, is the rubric assigned to the document, which in itself provides an indication of the way the lower levels should respond to its contents.

The boundaries between different types of documents as indicated by different rubrics are somewhat fuzzy and permeable, especially given the fact that the Central leaders have available more than fifteen such titles (such as ming-ling, chih-shih, chüeh-ting, etc.) that they can assign.[39] The continuum of meanings conveyed by these rubrics is broad enough, however, that it is important to be sensitive to differences among at least the major groups and what these mean to the recipients.

Every Central Document has a title,[40] and the specific rubric assigned to a document is based on a number of the characteristics of the contents of the CD: whether it is detailed and concrete or relatively vague; whether or not it calls for experimentation by lower level organs; whether it is being used simply to convey reference materials, with some indication of the way to handle and read these materials; and so forth. At the same time, the assigned rubric may tell the receiving organ a good deal about the procedure gone through to draft the CD, how final and binding the contents of the document are, and how to handle the document. Thus, rubrics are important: they are assigned with care by the originating organ and are noted by the recipients. The rubrics, in turn, form a sort of continuum, from the most detailed and rigidly binding documents at the one end to the most tentative and provisional at the other. The following comments characterize what seem to be the most frequently used CD rubrics.

A ming-ling (order) demarcates the detailed and binding end of this continuum. It brooks no local deviation in implementation (unless, of course, some specific provision in the ming-ling text itself calls for adaptation to local conditions). A ming-ling represents the conclusion of the full drafting process at the Center and thus is not considered in any way provisional. As such, local leaders may not question its wisdom when they receive it--rather, they may only discuss how best to implement it so that their actions conform with not only the spirit but also the letter of the document. The Cultural Revolution provided us with a number of examples of ming-ling, most of which tended to be concerned with military affairs.[41]

Because ming-ling are intended to be implemented quite precisely, they are typically assigned to documents whose contents are specific and concrete. It is simply inappropriate to issue a ming-ling to deal, for instance, with the changing scope of an ongoing political campaign, for a directive on a political campaign by its very nature requires flexible implementation according to local conditions.

A chüeh-ting (decision) occupies the next major slot on the continuum from binding to tentative rubrics.[42] Chüeh-ting are, like ming-ling, considered as authoritative conclusions of the Central authorities, reached after full consideration of the question concerned. They are, therefore, to be implemented rather than tested and questioned. A chüeh-ting differs from a ming-ling mainly in that it tends to allow a bit more play in its implementation. This is the rubric of choice, then, for documents that represent strong Central decisions but where the nature of the question demands that the decision be stated in somewhat more general terms, and some greater flexibility be allowed in adapting the decision to local conditions in the process of implementation. Not infrequently, therefore, chüeh-ting are used for documents that deal with developments in major political campaigns.[43] In the Cultural Revolution, many chüeh-ting stipulated the Center's decisions on the developments in various provinces both for the benefit of the principals concerned and as references for other provinces.[44]

Kuei-ting (regulations) define the next point on the continuum and indeed seem to straddle the line between two major groups of CDs: those that require relatively strict implementation and those that require lower levels to grasp and implement the spirit rather than the letter of the document. Some kuei-ting make clear that the letter of the document must be followed (such as the regulations promulgated on the Sinkiang production and construction corps in February 1967),[45] while others explicitly stress that it is only the spirit of the document that lower level actions must embody (such as the Central Committee's ten regulations on grasping revolution and promoting production).[46]

A chih-shih (instruction), one of the most commonly used rubrics, has clearly slipped across the line into the group of documents that permit lower levels flexibility in implementing the spirit of the document rather than requiring them to follow to the letter the text of the CD. A unit receiving a chih-shih typically investigates local conditions in order to devise appropriate means of carrying out the spirit of the Central directive in the local area. The local unit's plan for implementing the CD is then submitted to higher authorities for approval, after which it is activated. Thus, while both chih-shih and chüeh-ting can deal with issues that require some local adaptation (and therefore the line between them is not always obvious to the outsider), the two types of documents are relatively distinctive in their degree of authoritativeness.

A t'ung-chih (circular) is often the rubric of choice for a CD that is used as a cover letter to circulate reference materials. This cover letter, as indicated above, usually states what the materials are, how they should be handled, and the main points to which one should pay attention when reading them. By way of example, the major group of materials on the Lin Piao affair mentioned above was sent out under a t'ung-chih rubric, although a CD starting up a campaign to criticize Lin Piao would more likely be labeled either chih-shih or chüeh-ting.

Perhaps most tentative is the group of CDs that bear the rubric i-chien (opinion). This title makes clear that these are the initial views of the Center on a subject and that more information is necessary before any final decision can be reached. An i-chien, therefore, is regarded as a call for discussion and for carrying out investigations and experiments, the results of which should be reported back up the hierarchy to be used in the final decision making process on the issue concerned. Presumably, then, an i-chien permits the lower levels a somewhat greater degree of latitude in discussing the document--i.e., the lower level units may be able to express opinions about the basic spirit of the CD rather than confining themselves to its concrete particulars. An i-chien, in brief, indicates that the Center has not yet made a decision on an issue and wants to raise the problem for discussion. The "opinion" of the Central Committee concerning the Great Proletarian Cultural Revolution in the middle schools, issued in February 1967, for example, was issued only for "discussion and experimentation."[47]

Thus, Central Documents are given specific labels and these signal to the recipients within somewhat broad limits the degree to which the document represents the finished product of Central deliberations as opposed to the tentative opinions of the Central leadership before any final decision has been reached. The same rubrics inform the local unit of the rough degree to which it can exercise discretion in adapting the substance of the CD to local conditions for purposes of implementation.

One possibly misleading label is that of a "draft" (ts'ao-an). Once passed by the Central Committee and circulated as a CD, the "draft" rubric does not indicate that the decisions contained therein are either tentative or for local adaptation. Rather, the ts'ao-an label is typically applied to documents for which the problem under scrutiny is relatively new and where there is, consequently, relatively little information available on which to base a long-term program. Thus, although the authorities have reached a firm decision, they recognize that there is a good chance that the decision will have to be modified at some point in the future due either to changing conditions or the availability of new and important information. The "Sixty Points on People's Communes," for instance, which appeared initially as a draft and later as a revised draft,[48] assumed a "draft" form because it concerned a subject on which the PRC's historical experience was quite limited. The treatment of such a "draft" by local units is determined by the rubric (chih-shih, kuei-ting, etc.) assigned to the document in addition to the "ts'ao-an" label.[49] The ts'ao-an presents a particularly confusing wrinkle since many CDs actually circulate in "draft" form before they are passed officially and sent as CDs. The comments above, therefore, refer only to those "drafts" that have actually been adopted and circulated as part of the numbered series of Central Documents.

The CD "draft" thus has authority behind it and is expected to be implemented in full accord with the rubric given it. During the course of implementation, however, there is a constant stream of reporting back,[50] which gradually gives the authorities the data necessary to reach a longer-term set of decisions about the problem concerned. When appropriate, the Center may at a subsequent time issue a "revised draft," which in turn also enjoys the full authority of a Central decision. This was true, for instance, of several of the major documents in the Socialist Education Campaign that were passed in 1963-64, where the draft regulations for the campaign issued in September 1963 (the so-called "Later Ten Points") were replaced a year later by the revised draft regulations (called the "Revised Later Ten Points").[51]

Lastly, the t'ung-pao (notification) rubric is typically assigned to CDs that are used either to criticize and repudiate or to commend a particular person, unit, or example. A t'ung-pao from the Central Committee calls for public attention, study, or a serious warning--it is not a matter to be taken lightly.

The above list does not exhaust the types of rubrics that the Center may place on a CD, but it does cover the ones most frequently employed. Most of the others tend to cluster around one or another of the rubrics listed above and may be very difficult to distinguish from them in terms of the information conveyed by the rubric to the receiving organ.[52]

Indeed, the dividing line between even some of the major rubrics does not appear to be hard and fast. Thus, for instance, the critical

Central Document of 16 May 1966, which announced the purge of Yang Shang-k'un, Lu Ting-i, Chou Yang, and P'eng Chen, and marked a major escalatory step on the way to the Cultural Revolution, carried a t'ung-chih label, while the Central Committee's decision on launching the GPCR assumed the form of a chih-shih.[53] Nevertheless, the rubric assigned does convey to the receiving units some general information concerning the degree to which the document represents well-considered decisions of the Center and the flexibility permitted in implementing them. It makes all the difference, to cite a relatively extreme example, whether a particular CD is given the rubric ming-ling or i-chien. In this case, the response of the receiving units would differ immensely based only on the rubrics assigned.

In broad terms, one can group the rubrics discussed above into three major categories: those requiring implementation of the letter as well as the spirit of the document; those requiring implementation only of the spirit; and those used primarily to cite examples or provide reference materials. Most Central Documents seem to fall into the latter two categories. Put differently, the majority of CDs are not detailed orders that the Central authorities expect the receiving units to carry out to the letter. Rather, CDs typically permit (and assume) considerable flexibility in how local units handle them. The receiving organs may not violate the spirit of these documents, for that would be construed as "forming independent kingdoms." They may, however, adapt the substance of the documents to local levels--which allows, as explained below, considerable room for policy making in the process of policy implementation. If the receiving unit believes that the "spirit" of the CD is inappropriate given the local situation, it is obligated to present this dissenting opinion to the higher authorities and ask for instructions. At the same time, however, the principle of democratic centralism demands that the unit carry out the "spirit" of the document concerned until it has been relieved of this obligation by the higher authorities.

Levels of Classification for Central Documents. The level of classification of a document also determines the way it is handled by the issuing and receiving units. A minority of Central Documents are unclassified, and the documents themselves state that their contents are to be posted in public places. For instance, a CD of 1 December 1966 concerning the question of exchange of revolutionary experience by revolutionary teachers and students concluded with the statement: "This circular may be read out among the revolutionary teachers and students of universities and middle schools, and put up in organs and schools and at railway stations and wharves."[54] This use of CDs to communicate directly with the public was more characteristic of the Cultural Revolution--when other communication links between the leaders and the masses broke down--than of other periods.

Most Central Documents bear one of three levels of classification, and all such documents require special handling. No classified document may be communicated directly to the public (although, as explained below in the section on the transmission [ch'uan-ta] process, the spirit of portions of classified documents may be communicated to the public). These documents also may not be sent via the regular postal service, and post office officials have the right (and obligation) to refuse to handle any classified material. Each of these documents must be delivered by special courier.[55] In addition, each copy of a classified CD is individually numbered so that every one can be accounted for. The circulation of most CDs is, therefore, closely controlled.

There are distinctions among the three levels of classification applied to these documents. The first type, mi-chien (secret documents), contains general secrets. The second classification, chi-mi (institutional secrets), contains classified information pertinent to the institution classifying the document. The third classification, chüeh-mi (absolutely secret), is used for the most sensitive information. Chüeh-mi documents are therefore controlled by special procedures for issuance, dissemination and reception by a local unit. Typically, every copy must be returned to the issuing institution within a specified period of time. Even cadres who are Party members, except those with the appropriate special clearance, are not allowed to see these chüeh-mi documents.

Variations in the Use of CDs versus Other Forms of Bureaucratic Communications. One additional dimension of variation stands out in any review of Central Documents--that is, the changing use of these documents in relation to other forms of bureaucratic communications in the PRC over the years. That there has been considerable variation in this area is strongly suggested by impressive differences in the frequency with which CDs have been issued during different years. These documents are numbered serially, beginning with number one each new calendar year, and thus it is possible to specify the average rate of output of these documents each year. Since the documentation available in the West typically does not include the final Central Document for each year, analysts can only guess at the total annual output but can pinpoint quite accurately changes in the rate of monthly output over time. The results are striking, as indicated in table 1.

TABLE 1
CENTRAL DOCUMENTS AVAILABLE IN THE WEST

Year	Total Number of CDs	Highest CD Number and Date		Average Number per Month
1966*	25		n.a.	n.a.
1967	97	396	12/22/67	40
1968	19	94	6/15/68	17.1
1969	5	55	8/28/69	6.9
1970	6	56	9/12/70	6.6
1971	8	82	12/26/71	6.8
1972	5	25	9/72	2.9
1973	1	34	9/8/73	4.1
1974	6	26	10/74 (approx.)	2.7
1975	4		n.a.	n.a.
1976	12	24	12/10/76	1.9
1977	13	15	5/3/77	3.3

Note: All of these Central Documents are listed in Appendix II of this volume.

* Although Central Documents were numbered before 1966, none of the serial numbers of the pre-GPCR documents is available outside China. This table, therefore, must begin with 1966.

The above table brings several points into sharp relief. First, if the rate of CD output in the early 1960s approximated that given above for the 1970s, then the Cultural Revolution produced a great, albeit temporary, increase in the number of CDs issued. Why should this have been the case? In part, at the height of the disruption of the Cultural Revolution, when almost all other forms of bureaucratic links between the Center and the locales had been severed or impaired,[56] the Central Documents were made to do heavy duty by being used for a large variety of communications that in normal times would have gone through other channels. This broadened use of CDs was highlighted by the fact that many of these Central Documents bore the imprimatur of the State Council, Military Affairs Committee, and/or Cultural Revolution Group in addition to that of the Central Committee. Also, given the shattering of bureaucratic authority and personalization of legitimacy in Mao Tse-tung characteristic of these years, the leadership in Peking may well have felt a need to grace a maximum range of communications with the seal of approval of Chairman Mao--a task that could be accomplished most effectively through the vehicle of issuing documents in the name of the "Party Center," which at that time was clearly identified with the person of the Chairman.[57] This meant, then, that CDs were used during this time both to do yeoman service in terms of intrabureaucratic communications, carrying information that would normally have gone through other channels, and to communicate with the masses, putting Mao Tse-tung's authority behind directives that concerned a wide range of issues of direct relevance to mass participation in the Cultural Revolution. Lastly, the bulge in CDs during this period quite clearly reflects the fact that the Cultural Revolution thrust to the fore the types of issues that, as noted earlier, were the logical subject for CDs--i.e., political issues of broad consequence in an ongoing campaign. All these factors undoubtedly contributed to the swelling number of Central Documents as the Cultural Revolution peaked--and to the rather steady decline in the number of CDs as the force of the GPCR ebbed.

During 1968 the People's Liberation Army assumed a steadily expanding share of the national administrative burden. This process of reconstituting alternative bureaucratic links between the Center and the locales probably accounts for most of the decrease in the number of CDs issued in 1968 versus 1967. Indeed, probably only the continuing importance of Cultural Revolution related issues--such as the rehabilitation of cadres and the formation of provincial and municipal Party committees--during 1969-71 kept the average number of CDs per month slightly higher in these years than would be the case later.

After 1971 the volume of CDs remains rather constant at roughly three per month. The one year for which this proved not to be the case was 1976, when the number for the entire year fell to an average of less than two per month. Indeed, even this figure is somewhat inflated, as the purge of the Gang of Four on 6 October spurred the issuance of several CDs[58] that brought the overall average for the year up to a level somewhat higher than that which characterized the first nine months of this period. Central Document #1 of 1976, for instance, was not issued until 3 February.[59] Thus, the tremendous political strife that characterized the leadership during 1976 evidently combined with the increasing frailty of Party Chairman Mao Tse-tung to paralyze to a degree the Party Center's ability to make authoritative decisions and communicate them to lower levels.[60] Additionally, given the purge of Teng Hsiao-p'ing in early April following on the heels of the T'ien An Men incident and the subsequent debate over the scope and methods of the campaign to criticize Teng,[61] it seems virtually certain that a number of the CDs issued during this year of political turmoil must have concerned essentially issues of factional politics at the Center rather than provided clear guidance on how to handle problems in various areas of China's society and economy.

Unfortunately, the available information does not permit us to specify whether or not the decline in the rate of issuance of CDs in fact began as early as 1975. It is in July-September of that year that Teng Hsiao-p'ing is accused of making a major bid to consolidate his position and undermine the radicals, causing the latter to place still greater urgency on weakening Teng before Chou En-lai's demise. This radical counteroffensive, in turn, produced the Water Margin political campaign and open political conflict at the (First) National Conference on Learning from Tachai in September-October. Overall, then, the CD system may have reflected numerically a deterioration in the ability of the Politburo to reach authoritative decisions on the major problems confronting China for more than a year prior to Mao Tse-tung's death. The case studies on the key programmatic documents of 1975 on industry and on science and technology presented below strongly suggest that this was the case.

* * * * * * *

In sum, the Central Document series is a very pliable instrument for communications between the Party Center and the lower levels of the political system. It has been used not only to convey decisions, but also to circulate materials, give certain issues increased exposure, and so forth. Indeed, perhaps a majority of CDs either do not communicate decisions or allow for considerable flexibility in implementing the tasks they specify. The roles of Central Documents and their contents, moreover, have reflected changes in the composition and functions of the Politburo itself. This system of Central Documents has been, in brief, a bureaucratic instrument closely attuned to the political needs of the Party leadership and reflective of the changing relations of these leaders to the political system as a whole and to each other.

II. DRAFTING CENTRAL DOCUMENTS

There are really two dimensions to the question of how documents that are circulated as CDs are drafted: Why is an issue slated for communication via a CD in the first place? Having made the decision to put out a document on a particular problem, how is that document actually drafted and adopted?

Slating an Issue for Inclusion in a Central Document

We have dealt with this question briefly above, but it now warrants fuller treatment. The three major rationales for using a Central Document are political, bureaucratic and substantive. These are not completely mutually exclusive, but each does provide a distinctive logic for channeling an issue into the CD document flow.

From Mao Tse-tung's perspective, the Central Document system provided a means for routing all key political decisions across his desk for his personal approval before they could be communicated in the name of the Central Committee. In 1953, as noted in the Introduction, Mao laid down the stipulation that, "henceforth, no documents and telegrams that use the name of the Central Committee may be issued without my having seen them or else they are invalid."[62] There is no record of his ever having cancelled this order and much evidence to suggest that it remained in effect--even with respect to those Central Documents that were later said during the Cultural Revolution to have violated Mao's policy prescriptions.

Perhaps the most famous (or infamous) example of the latter is the "February Outline Report"--a document drafted under the aegis of P'eng Chen in early February 1966 and approved for circulation by a meeting of the Politburo convened by Liu Shao-ch'i in Mao Tse-tung's absence. This "Report" declared that the extremely sensitive set of issues raised by the Wu Han affair called for academic criticism and should not be treated as a major political question.[63] At the time the "February Outline Report" was drafted and circulated, Chiang Ch'ing and Lin Piao teamed up to produce their own counterdocument, the "Summary of the Forum on Literature and Art for Troops." This "Summary" was finally adopted (and the "February Outline Report" repudiated) at the May 1966 Central Work Conference that also sanctioned the purge of P'eng Chen, Lu Ting-i, Yang Shang-k'un, and Lo Jui-ch'ing.[64]

Even the "February Outline Report," as it turns out, was presented to and approved by Chairman Mao before its dissemination. Red Guards subsequently revealed that P'eng Chen and some of the other drafters of the "Report" made a special trip to Wuchang on 7-8 February 1966 to present the "Report" to Mao and secure his consent for its circulation. The Red Guards contend that P'eng pulled the wool over the Chairman's eyes by presenting him with an inaccurate summary of the main points of the "Report" rather than showing him the document itself. They also assert that P'eng then returned to Peking claiming that Mao had specifically approved the "Report" for circulation when in fact the Chairman had done no such thing.[65] Regardless of the accuracy of this latter accusation, the important point is that as late as 1966 P'eng Chen had to submit this Central Document to Chairman Mao--even though the Party leader was in central China and the drafters of the document seemingly had strong incentives to try to steer it around him--before the document could be circulated under the imprimatur of the Central Committee.

Some other CDs available include Mao Tse-tung's comments on them, indicating clearly that he personally perused and approved them.[66] Informants suggest that these comments from the Chairman in fact typically graced CDs, even though the texts of the vast majority of these documents that are available in the West lack the Chairman's notations. Thus, Mao Tse-tung sculpted the Central Document system at least in part as a way of placing himself directly astride the key communications from the Party Center to other units.

The widespread belief in China that all CDs had been signed off personally by Chairman Mao[67] clearly created a somewhat different type of political imperative for some policy advocates, for if they could embody key components of their views in a CD, then Mao's personal authority had been placed behind their stance on the issue in question. Thus, a member of the Politburo might try to route an issue into the Central Document stream precisely to give it an imprimatur of authority that would have been lacking had the document been issued by some other Party or government unit.

P'eng Chen's strategy on the "February Outline Report" represents a successful application of this strategy, at least for the short run. Yao Wen-yuan is said to have tried to apply the same tactic in early 1975, but ultimately failed. As of the winter-spring of 1975, the Gang of Four is accused of having tried to launch a campaign around the issue of "opposing empiricism," which presumably would have given them added ammunition to use against those cadres in the Party and army who paid too much attention to practical concerns at the expense of giving a leading role to theory. Initially, the Gang used its leverage over the PRC media to run articles on the importance of opposing empiricism, but they quickly judged that they had to have "opposing empiricism" specified in a Central Document if they were ever to be able to launch a major campaign around this issue. Their strategy was simple. Yao Wen-yuan took a Hsinhua News Agency draft document of 23 February 1975 that provided guidance to lower levels on how to report the current campaign to study the theory of the dictatorship of the proletariat and suggested that Hsinhua revise the draft so as to include mention of the need to "oppose empiricism." Yao then sent the draft to be read and approved by Chairman Mao so that it could be sent out as a Central Document. Mao read this document on 23 April 1975 but did not simply express his approval of it, as Yao had hoped. Rather, the Chairman noted on the document that the formulation about empiricism should be changed to a stricture against revisionism, which includes both empiricism and dogmatism--thus foiling Yao's attempt to place the Chairman on record against empiricism as the major danger as of early 1975. It bears noting that the subsequent Hsinhua News Agency account of this incident clearly outlined Yao's political strategy as one of channeling an issue into the CD stream in order to give it greater legitimacy and force than it otherwise could have enjoyed.[68]

There is also a political imperative for the entire Central leadership to use the CD format when they want to bring their collective authority to bear on an issue in order to put the issue at a suitably high place on the agenda of other units. As noted before, this political consideration probably played a central role in the use of CDs during the Cultural Revolution when the entire system suffered a power deflation and it was felt necessary to bring the authority of the "Center" to bear in order to give orders added force.

The <u>bureaucratic imperative</u> for channeling issues into the Central Document stream recognizes that the administrative regulations concerning communication between units in the bureaucracy prohibit a specialized agency at the Center (for example, the Agriculture and Forestry Political Department) from sending documents directly to a territorial committee at a lower level (for example, a hsien Party committee). Yet, clearly many of the directives of the Central Committee department in charge of agriculture[69] require the active cooperation of the local Party committees in order to be carried out effectively, as these directives may require that appropriate arrangements be made regarding transport, propaganda, the allocation of labor, and so forth. The hsien Party committee's Agriculture and Forestry Department can (and should) provide the hsien Party committee with a copy of any important orders that have come down to it via the agriculture and forestry system, but each Party committee receives copies of hundreds of such orders to its specialized departments and need not pay them much heed. Thus, the advantage of sending this directive down via the CD channel is that it makes it the responsibility of the hsien Party committee and requires that the Party committee make appropriate arrangements for the accomplishment of this multidimensional task.[70] Depending on the nature of the problem, it would also of course have been possible to have the appropriate State Council Ministry route the directive through the State Council document series so as to give it appropriate priority among the tasks of the hsien revolutionary committee (or, before the GPCR, the hsien people's council).

Presumably, the Party versus the government channel is chosen as a function of the importance the Central leadership assigns to the task, the need to tap Party resources (such as the more extensive Party presence at the basic levels in the countryside) in addition to the government bureaucracy in order to carry out the task properly, the perceived political as opposed to purely technical components of the task, and the current general balance among the Party, government, and army bureaucracies in the system. Frequently, the combined political/technical nature of such a document is given recognition by having the Central Committee and the State Council jointly sponsor it (although it is issued as a part of the CD document series in these instances).

The October 1960 "Directive of the CCP Central Committee and the State Council on the Launching of a Vigorous Mass Campaign for Collection and Purchase of Autumn Farm Products"[71] exemplifies this type of CD. The heart of the directive concerns a technical government function--the State procurement of products from the fall harvest. In fact, however, proper accomplishment of this task, according to the CD, requires that the following dimensions of rural work be done well: "harvesting, distribution, collection and purchase, work connected with the arrangement of the livelihood of rural residents, processing, and transportation. [These tasks in turn require] intensive carrying out of ideological work, organization of preparatory work in various fields, estimation of crop yields in a down-to-earth manner, rational assignment of tasks, and arrangement and transfer of labor where necessary."[72] Thus, it would be inadequate to send this directive out only via the agriculture and forestry bureaucratic system, as its implementation requires that other functional sectors give related tasks high priority. At the same time, the political dimensions of this technical task are substantial, requiring large-scale mobilization and organization of rural labor and the resolution of such sticky problems as income distribution during a year of poor harvests. Thus, both the nature of the task and the formal administrative rules concerning channeling of documents within the Chinese bureaucracy greatly enhanced the chances that in this instance a Central Document would be used to accomplish the seemingly technical state function of agricultural procurement.

The substantive imperative for issuing a Central Document materializes when the leadership must deal with an important issue that is not the specific responsibility of any particular functional part of the bureaucracy. Again, if the issue were purely administrative in nature, it could be handled via a State Council directive on the government side or a document from the General Office of the CCP on the Party side.[73] Directives concerning the carrying out of a major political campaign and those discussing or providing information on sensitive current political problems reflect the demands of the substantive imperative.

The many CDs concerning how to carry out the Great Proletarian Cultural Revolution[74] exemplify this substantive rationale for a Central Document. The numerous CDs noted above[75] that conveyed information about the Lin Piao affair likewise dealt with a problem of high political sensitivity that was not in the province of any particular functional unit. During the winter-spring of 1976-77, the rehabilitation of Teng Hsiao-p'ing best typified the type of issue that would have to be handled via CDs as opposed to other forms of bureaucratic communications.[76] It is not surprising, therefore, that at least four Central Documents dealt with this issue during these months.[77] In a similar vein, other major rehabilitation questions growing out of the Cultural Revolution have most likely produced pertinent CDs over the years since 1969, although none of these is available. Thus, the very fact that an issue is of political importance and is not in the domain of a functionally specialized hierarchy may alone be sufficient to provide the impetus that propels the issue into the Central Document stream.

Having determined to use the Central Document system to deal with an issue, how are the pertinent Central Documents drafted and adopted?[78]

Do these documents typically represent the collective judgment of the Party Center, or can they reflect the views of a minority and be issued without collective consultation involving all members of the Politburo? How are the texts of these documents drafted, and to what extent are they debated and discussed before being approved? What kind of documentary trail is left by this drafting process? What is the strategy followed by individual leaders who want to have a CD put out that focuses on a particular topic of concern to them? How does the CD drafting and adoption process mesh with what analysts have already learned previously about the consultative process at the highest levels of the Party? And what dimensions of this process are subject to political manipulation? The following section addresses these important and interrelated issues.

The Drafting and Adoption Processes

Given the variety of types of Central Documents, it is not surprising to find considerable variations in the drafting process. Most likely, some of these documents have been issued over the years on Mao Tse-tung's personal authority,[79] especially those that consist merely of an instruction by Mao that a document sent to the Central Committee should be given wider circulation.[80] In this case, the Chairman almost certainly simply passed this instruction along to the Party Secretariat (before the Cultural Revolution) or the General Office (after the Cultural Revolution), where his directive was put into proper form, chopped, and circulated with the item he wanted sent around attached as an appendix.[81]

Other CDs pose more complex problems of drafting. Some, such as the series of documents on the Lin Piao affair, probably require a great deal of discussion concerning what items should be circulated as appendices and some additional consultation concerning the instructions on studying and transmitting these items that are included in the CD cover letter itself. The actual drafting of the CD in these instances, by contrast, is probably relatively simple and pro forma. Other CDs, by contrast, either deal with more specialized areas, where consultation with the specialized bureaucratic bodies is necessary in order to produce a good document, or they concern major programmatic statements that have wide ramifications. Both of these latter types of documents (and they are not completely mutually exclusive) entail a more complex drafting process. The following pages portray this process first in skeletal form and then via case studies of two major documents.

The Chinese Politburo is basically divided into two tiers: several top leaders, usually members of the Standing Committee, act as generalists; and the majority of the Politburo members assume responsibility for supervising the affairs of one or several particular functional areas under the "division of responsibility system" (fen-kung chih-tu).[82] While any generalist may concern himself with various issue areas as his interests, talents, and relations with his colleagues permit, other members of the Politburo are not allowed to intervene directly in the affairs of a functional area beyond their assigned sphere of activity. For substantively important CDs and those concerning complicated topics, typically a member of the Politburo with special responsibility for the functional area concerned assumes responsibility for drafting the CD. For instance, during the period of consolidation following the Great Leap Forward, Po I-po took charge of drafting the "Seventy Points on Industry," Li Hsien-nien formulated the "Sixty Points on Finance and Banking," and Lu Ting-i assumed responsibility for drafting the "Eight Articles on Literature and Art."[83] Each was a major programmatic document in its field. In similar fashion, Hua Kuo-feng, who assumed responsibility for science and technology following the Fourth National People's Congress in January 1975, took part in the process of drafting the major programmatic document in that field, the "Outline Summary Report of the Work of the Academy of Sciences."[84]

There is, however, room for political maneuvering within this system of assigning Central Documents to the Politburo member who has the major responsibility for that functional area. One strategy is for a Politburo member to utilize his prerogatives to establish a legitimate claim to an issue that would not normally fall into his bailiwick. In early 1966, for example, Lin Piao was constructing a coalition that would help him brush aside many of the leading cadres of the Party. One of his targets was P'eng Chen, who ranked among the five most powerful men in the country. P'eng, however, had begun to experience serious difficulties over his close ties with Wu Han, who in turn had come under attack for writing Hai Jui Dismissed from Office. Part of P'eng's self-defense strategy was to confine the definition of Wu Han's transgression to the field of culture and education. He accomplished this first by instructing that all articles criticizing Hai Jui be sent to Lu Ting-i, P'eng's colleague and the candidate Politburo member in charge of culture,[85] and then by drafting and having adopted the CD subsequently referred to as the "February Outline Report."[86] To join the attack on P'eng Chen, therefore, Lin Piao had to devise a legitimate means for engaging an issue in this field, which he accomplished by appointing Chiang Ch'ing cultural advisor to the PLA and putting her in charge of a "Forum on Literature and Art for Troops." Chiang Ch'ing's "Forum Summary," which she repeatedly discussed with her husband, attacked the basic points of the "February Outline Report" and, after considerable political maneuvering, was adopted as official policy in May 1966.[87] Almost ten years later, Chiang Ch'ing engaged in a similar maneuver to gain leverage over foreign trade. In 1975 she used her position as cultural tsar to launch criticism of the Chinese arts and crafts that were being exported. Having gained this entering wedge into the foreign trade arena, she then tried to enlarge her prerogatives there by raising issues that could affect China's entire import and export policy.[88]

The impetus for drafting a Central Document to deal with a particular problem area can come from several sources. Often a remark by Mao Tse-tung indicating that policy toward a certain issue had to be clarified would be enough to initiate the drafting process. The other Politburo "generalists" seem also to have enjoyed this power. On a more technical issue area, the initiative may actually come from the State Council (formerly via Chou En-lai; currently most likely via Hua Kuo-feng or Teng Hsiao-p'ing), which will raise a problem that requires high level attention and guidance. The impetus for the "Outline Summary Report on the Work of the Academy of Sciences" in 1975 came, for instance, from a State Council report in late 1974 that argued that work in the Academy had to be consolidated and its leadership strengthened. Mao Tse-tung approved the report. From there, Teng Hsiao-p'ing evidently took overall charge of the issue and assigned Hua Kuo-feng to play a role in it.[89] In this instance, the circle is completed by the fact that as a man who was playing an increasingly important role in the work of the State Council during the course of 1974, Teng may well have inspired the State Council report in the first place. Alternatively, Chou En-lai may have initiated the report in consultation with Teng.

A Politburo member or alternate who controls a specific issue area seems to be able to initiate the drafting of a CD concerning that area on his own authority, although he cannot actually promulgate the document as a CD without higher level sanction. Lu Ting-i, for instance, carried through the drafting of the "Eight Points on Literature and Art" without evident approval from any top-ranking Politburo member.[90] The only strict prohibition seems to be against having a person draft a CD in an issue area for which he has no officially assigned responsibility. The Chinese authorities have asserted, for instance, that Chiang Ch'ing had to resort to a "poem-report" on the Paracel Island victory in 1974 because she lacked the authority to write an official "report" on anything in the strictly military sphere.[91]

Each leading Politburo member evidently has a staff of personal advisors, and one or more of these may play a role in the drafting of a document in which the Politburo member is involved. Once the person on the Politburo[92] with responsibility for a specific functional area takes over the drafting process, moreover, he typically contacts people in the appropriate executive organs and assigns them the task of pulling together the data necessary for drafting the CD.[93] This in turn initiates a process of consultation, research and investigation that might well stretch down to the basic levels, if this is felt necessary. The consultation involves sounding out people in the appropriate functional hierarchy at lower levels of the bureaucracy to solicit their views on the current situation and how best to handle the problem on the agenda. Frequently meetings are convened at various levels to discuss the issue. Research includes checking appropriate documentation on previous policy, technical documentary material relevant to finding the best solution to the problem concerned, and, prudently, Mao's known statements relevant to the issue. Often investigations are commissioned as a part of this process,[94] either to generate better data on real conditions in the problem area concerned or to trial test some of the proposed solutions so as to provide the leadership with data on the likely results of the proposals. These investigations may well produce models for later use. Some available data strongly suggest that particular Politburo members cultivate individual locales where they return repeatedly to test out proposed policies--evidently because they know the local situation relatively well and have faith in the local leaders' integrity, wisdom, and loyalty.[95] Through this process of consultation, investigation, and research, an initial draft is produced.

This initial draft is then sent to the person on the Politburo who commissioned the document, and this person must sign off on it before it can be put up for formal adoption. If the person is completely satisfied with the draft, he signs his name in a box at the top of the document marked <u>shen-p'i jen</u> (examiner) or <u>p'i-fa jen</u> (censor) and adds his affirmative comments in the space provided. The draft is then ready for final adoption, chopping, and transmission to lower levels for implementation.

Frequently, however, the Politburo person in charge wants to discuss some details of the draft and perhaps suggest some revisions. A commonly used vehicle for this is the "report meeting" (<u>hui-pao hui-i</u>), for which he may gather together some of his key advisors and people who have played important roles in drafting the document. At this meeting, the Politburo member first listens to a report on the drafting process and its results, possibly interjecting comments here and there during the presentation. He then stimulates discussion of the issues that continue to concern him, indicating parts of the text that should be deleted and additional items that might be included. He may also request stylistic changes.[96] The document then goes back into the drafting process, where appropriate additional work is done on it. This may include any or all of the drafting steps mentioned above, depending upon the nature of the comments made during the <u>hui-pao</u> meeting.[97]

Once the draft has been rewritten, it is sent back to the responsible Politburo member, who again may convene a <u>hui-pao</u> meeting and make additional comments requiring yet another round of drafting changes. Indeed, it is not extraordinary for a major document to go through three or more major draftings before being accepted for formal promulgation.[98] Importantly, given the sharp reversals in Chinese politics over the past fifteen years, written records are kept of each of these drafts, of the discussion at each "report meeting" and other conferences convened during the drafting process, and of each set of comments written on the document by the Politburo member in charge. After the final document is promulgated, moreover, all of this material is filed together in the Party archives (controlled by the General Office of the CCP, headed by Yang Shang-k'un before the Cultural Revolution and by Wang Tung-hsing since 1966). Thus, this procedure leaves a document trail behind that allows people who have access to the archives to reconstruct each step of the process with some accuracy[99] at a later date.

In China as elsewhere, however, drafting a document is not equivalent to having it adopted as official policy. Again, considerable variation seems to characterize the adoption process, depending on the contents of the CD involved and the circumstances of its drafting. There is little doubt that, as noted above, Mao Tse-tung virtually on his own authority could use the Central Document format to send out material for reference to various localities. Similarly, it seems probable that functionally quite specific documents that were not highly controversial could be adopted with only the barest nod toward real consultation on the issue by the whole Politburo.[100] This is presumably the case because many items are too specialized to arouse the interest of most of the members. Indeed, perhaps specialized CDs could be put out by the person in charge of drafting with Mao's approval alone, rather than formally having to take this up with other members of the Politburo. It seems, in any case, that all Politburo members are apprised of the contents of all CDs, but relatively few of these documents engender considerable discussion and debate.

CDs that are broader in character or that deal with more controversial issues of the day are, however, subjected to protracted debate in a process that can become highly politicized. In these instances, policy advocates may use meetings convened during the drafting process as vehicles for mobilizing a constituency for their views. Where the issue is sufficiently broad that it overlaps the jurisdictions of several Politburo members, moreover, each might sponsor his own drafting process and bring policy papers with supporting information to the meeting convened to resolve the issue.

Examples of these tactics abound. At the summer 1962 Central Work Conference that convened in Peitaiho and Peking, for instance, Ch'en Po-ta gave the formal report on agriculture, which probably reflected Mao Tse-tung's views on the issue. Ch'en Yun raised a distinctively different set of views, perhaps in league with T'ao Chu, who had carried out his own investigations and came to the meeting with the data in hand to support Ch'en Yun's views.[101] To cite another example, during the early 1966 process of drafting and the competing "February Outline Report" and the "Summary of the Forum on Literature and Art for Troops" and then adopting first the "Outline" and then the "Summary" as official policy, each principal leader convened a range of meetings to flesh out his own ideas and mobilize support for his position. For P'eng Chen, these included meetings of the Five-Man Cultural Revolution Group, the Peking Municipal Party Committee, and the Standing Committee of the Peking Party Committee, all of which he headed. Liu Shao-ch'i convened the Standing Committee of the Politburo in Mao's absence, and the Party Chairman in turn called meetings of the Politburo Standing Committee, the full Politburo, and a Central Committee Conference. Lin Piao arranged a special military forum and convened meetings of the Military Affairs Committee, while Teng Hsiao-p'ing called together the Secretariat of the Central Committee. Many of these meetings, moreover, were "enlarged," indicating that the convener could manipulate the roster of participants to meet his political requirements and goals.[102]

A basic programmatic document, moreover, is often discussed and passed at a major national meeting such as a Central Work Conference. The Politburo does not usually present the rest of the Party with a fait accompli on issues of great importance.[103] These Central work conferences can be the scene of high drama, as is attested by the well-known battle between Mao Tse-tung and P'eng Teh-huai at the Lushan Conference of July 1959 and the tense confrontations at the January-February 1962 Seven Thousand Cadres Meeting, the July-September 1962 Peitaiho/Peking gathering, and the 4-18 May 1966 conclave that witnessed the purge of P'eng Chen, Lu Ting-i, Lo Jui-ch'ing, and Yang Shang-k'un and the adoption of the famous May 16th Circular.[104]

Preparation for these conferences often goes beyond the drafting of appropriate documents and policy papers, especially if the leaders are sharply split on fundamental issues. Provincial chiefs may fortify themselves for these gatherings by convening appropriate meetings at the regional or provincial level, while participants who work in the functional departments at the Center may convene functionally specialized meetings to gather the appropriate data. Even the Politburo-level participants, as noted above, might don one of the range of institutional hats most of them wear to gather together groups of advisors and use them to test out and refine their views.[105] While the meeting is in progress, furthermore, groups of administrators and specialists who are particularly concerned with the policy area under discussion may meet simultaneously and are called upon to serve both as a pool of available expertise and, perhaps, as a lobby in favor of one viewpoint or another at the major meeting.[106]

Thus, the arena in which wide-ranging, programmatic CDs are adopted is one that transcends the more formal drafting process outlined above and may vastly widen the range of people who have input, either directly or indirectly, into the final decision. The variety of political strategies to influence the outcome that can be brought to bear is virtually limitless and defies elegant description and categorization. Suffice it to note that once an issue enters the "meeting system" in China, it becomes part of an extraordinarily elaborate, flexible, and dynamic system where politics remains a high art.[107] The adoption of CDs that articulate major programmatic policies, therefore, differs greatly from that of CDs that are more narrowly focused, even though the drafting process for both types of Central Documents is similar in basic outline.

The above description of the drafting of Central Documents draws, as the notes indicate, on data from the mid-1950s to the mid-1970s. The continuities in the process over this twenty-year period are striking, with the exception only of the years of the Cultural Revolution and the tortured recovery from the ravages of that movement during the early

1970s. Another common feature of these years is that, with few exceptions, they mark a period when Teng Hsiao-p'ing played key roles in China's Party administrative system--as head of the Central Committee Secretariat until his ouster in the Cultural Revolution, and again as a central figure in the policy process during the years 1974 and 1975. Research already completed has provided analysts with a solid overview of the functioning of the administrative system during the years of Teng's ascendancy before the Cultural Revolution, even though this research was not explicitly focused on Teng and his administrative techniques.[108]

The following case studies focus on the drafting of two major programmatic documents under Teng Hsiao-p'ing's aegis when he was at the height of his power (albeit involved in a fight to enhance and retain that power) during 1975. These two documents were not adopted as CDs, for they became casualties of the attacks on Teng by Chiang Ch'ing and her colleagues in the fall of 1975. Both, however, were clearly intended to be Central Documents, and press reports from China make clear that they (perhaps in slightly revised form) became official policy during 1977.[109] Although the system as of 1975 was badly torn apart by factional strife, Teng's central role in the drafting of these critical documents makes them good cases to analyze in order to gain insight into how the Chinese Central Document system can be expected to function under the Hua Kuo-feng/Teng Hsiao-p'ing administration now in power. Overall, moreover, there are few surprises in the story of these two documents. Indeed, it is remarkable to see the basic continuity in the process of drafting major Central Documents that has characterized the Chinese policy process for more than two decades.[110]

The Drafting of Central Documents under Teng Hsiao-p'ing in 1975: Two Cases

China in 1975 was caught in the grip of "succession politics," i.e., the political maneuvering geared to securing positions for the imminent succession to Party Chairman Mao Tse-tung and Premier Chou En-lai dominated the political intercourse of the period. Teng Hsiao-p'ing had been rehabilitated in 1973, an event which in turn had greatly excited Peking politics. As the number two target of the Cultural Revolution and a man known for his toughness, Teng's return to the pinnacle of Chinese politics could only spell serious trouble for the radicals who had purged him in 1966 and still remained in power. Both sides realized, as Teng rapidly accumulated power in his hands during the course of 1973-75, that a showdown could not be avoided. In this situation, each side utilized the resources at its command to bolster its position, and each searched for allies in the political system.

Teng's approach was simple. Since no words or deeds could convince the radicals that he would not seek revenge, he decided to put himself in such a powerful position as of the time of Chou En-lai's death that he could survive any radical attack, no matter how severe, and retaliate in kind. During 1975, therefore, Teng was not centrally concerned with ameliorating conflict with the radicals. Rather, he sought to build bridges to potential allies through a clearly antiradical program: the four modernizations. Teng enjoyed Premier Chou En-lai's backing in this effort, although Chou had probably hoped to avoid a decisive rupture between Teng and the radicals after his death. Chou, in any event, was enfeebled by cancer and unable to carry on work on a sustained basis for almost the entire year.

Successful efforts to accomplish the four modernizations--i.e., the rapid modernization of industry, agriculture, the military, and science and technology--required an end to the political factionalism and instability that had plagued the Chinese system since the Cultural Revolution. They also demanded that clear priorities be established in each of these four key areas, with greater stress being put on discipline, output, and sustained effort than had been the case in recent years. Three major documents--the "Outline Summary Report on the Work of the Academy of Sciences,"[111] "On the General Program for the Work of the Party and the Country,"[112] and "On Certain Questions on Accelerating the Development of Industry"[113]--laid out Teng's fundamental approaches to the broad fields of science, the urban economy and foreign trade, the priorities for the national leadership, and the prickly issue of rectifying the country's political institutions. In content, indeed, these documents provide the most detailed and elaborate articulation available of Teng Hsiao-p'ing's plans in these major areas and, probably, on the substance of policy in 1977, since all three documents have been rehabilitated along with their sponsor. In the political context of 1975, these documents offered a powerful appeal to a range of potential Teng supporters in the succession: military leaders, scientists, older cadres, and all leaders anxious for the rapid development of China's economy.

All three of these major documents were drafted during July through October 1975, and their full political impact can be comprehended only by focusing on their content, grouping them together, and placing them in the context of other significant events of the period: Chou Jung-hsin's advocacy of policy changes in education; Teng Hsiao-p'ing's report to the National Conference on Learning from Tachai in Agriculture; and so forth. The object of the following case studies on the "Outline Summary Report on the Work of the Academy of Sciences" and "On Certain Questions on Accelerating the Development of Industry,"[114] however, is to illuminate the process of drafting these two articles rather than to analyze their substance and the political strategies of which they were a larger part.[115] Because of this focus on process, the present analysis treats each of these documents separately and makes only passing reference to the political context of which they were such an integral part. The following case studies of the drafting process (and the attempts to block passage of these documents by the radicals) do, nevertheless, highlight in stark terms both the different resources available to various participants by virtue of their assigned areas of responsibility in the Politburo and the effect of rules governing document drafting and document flow on political conflict and strategies in Peking.

The Outline Summary Report on the Work of the Academy of Sciences (hereafter abbreviated as "Outline Report"). The January 1975 Fourth National People's Congress had endorsed the program of the "four modernizations" as the central task for the government of the PRC for the remainder of the century.[116] During the course of the next ten months the Chinese leadership under Teng Hsiao-p'ing specified more concretely its plans to implement this general policy in each of the major areas concerned: agriculture, the military, science and technology, and industry. In all of these areas Party Chairman Mao Tse-tung gave supplemental instructions on the line that should be followed.[117] These instructions in turn provided the impetus for the drafting of specific policy programs in each sphere.[118]

In July 1975 Mao articulated a ten-point "thesis" on the proper set of priorities to pursue in the field of science and technology. This set of instructions emphasized the need to encourage the policy of letting one hundred flowers bloom and one hundred schools of thought contend so as to permit China to make greater advances in science.[119] It may well have been generated by a major military conference that had just met and laid down the policy to be adopted in this important sphere.[120] Clearly, military work and science and technology are sufficiently closely intertwined that major decisions in one could provide the impetus for directing attention toward the other.

On 18 July 1975, the Center sent a new leadership team to the Chinese Academy of Sciences to draft a major program for policy in the entire field of science and technology. Hu Yao-pang headed this new team, and he and his colleagues immediately set about drafting the "Outline Report." This group worked under a three-point charge from the Central authorities: to forge ahead firmly in overhauling[121] the Academy of Sciences; to strive rapidly to improve scientific work; and to submit a report to the Central Committee and the State Council as soon as possible after investigation and study.[122]

Hu Yao-pang and his colleagues immediately focused their attention on producing an initial discussion draft. Indeed, twenty of their first thirty days at the Academy were devoted exclusively to this effort, as they examined relevant documents from the files, conducted some investigations, and consulted with comrades inside and outside the Academy of Sciences.[123] As part of this effort, in late July one of the members of Hu's group met with the heads ("responsible comrades") of the science and technology departments in the Academy of Sciences.[124] By the end of July, Hu Yao-pang felt he had pulled enough information together to meet with Teng Hsiao-p'ing to give him an idea of the progress to date.

Hu and Teng held a hui-pao meeting on 1 August, at which time Hu related to Teng the contents of the draft report to date. Teng made comments and indicated his tentative approval, and this preliminary effort was then circulated to relevant personnel for their views. Objections were raised regarding some of the points, and appropriate revisions were made. Hu did not circulate this revised draft within the Academy, however, even to its Party core group. Rather, he sent it directly to Hu Ch'iao-mu, who at that time was serving on Teng's staff of personal advisors.[125] Hu Ch'iao-mu, in turn, commented on the draft and sent it back.[126]

On 17 August, Hu Yao-pang sent the revised draft (incorporating Hu Ch'iao-mu's comments ?) to Teng Hsiao-p'ing, along with a cover letter pointing out several key sections of the draft that had been revised according to instructions. The document itself was labeled a "Summary Report, First Discussion Draft," and extensive excerpts from it are available.[127] Nine days later, on 26 August, Teng assigned the task of further revisions to Hu Ch'iao-mu.

On 27 August, Teng met with Hu Ch'iao-mu and Hu Yao-pang and gave them concrete instructions for this next major revision of the draft.

During the time between Teng's receipt of the 17 August draft and this meeting, Mao Tse-tung had issued one of his periodic statements that allowed the radicals to raise a ruckus in the Chinese media. This was Mao's comment on the problem of capitulationism in the book The Water Margin.[128] Consequently, Teng told Hu Ch'iao-mu and Hu Yao-pang on 27 August that, while retaining all of the principles (i.e., substantive positions) of the 17 August draft, they should shorten the text, smooth out the political rough edges, and improve the writing. Teng commented that the drafting group should not consider itself to be Sung Chiang and should not "mistake the wind for the rain and imagine that things might go wrong." Hu Ch'iao-mu, nevertheless, recommended that the draft be rewritten so as to include a liberal sprinkling of the phraseology that had come into vogue after the Cultural Revolution, to which Teng agreed.[129]

Enter Hua Kuo-feng--or, is this the right time to bring Hua on stage? The problem arises because the various sources on the drafting process for the "Outline Report" clearly highlight the degree to which Chinese "revelations" of previous events are themselves biased and selective. The radicals' critique of this document, issued in April 1976 when Teng Hsiao-p'ing had just been purged and Hua Kuo-feng had just assumed the premiership and Party first vice-chairmanship, focuses on Teng's role in the drafting process to the total neglect of Hua's involvement. Reviews of the two-line struggle in scientific and technology work that were published in March 1977, when the leadership was trying energetically to build up Hua Kuo-feng's reputation, give Hua the sole leading role for work in this sphere in 1975.[130] On the eve of Teng Hsiao-p'ing's rehabilitation in July 1977, however, the leadership portrayed the history of the drafting of this document in terms of the involvement of Mao Tse-tung, Hua Kuo-feng, and "another leading comrade" or "another vice-premier,"[131] clearly meaning the still-unmentionable Teng Hsiao-p'ing. Thus, specifying the precise division of labor in this process is simply not possible. Indeed, given the fact that the most extensive materials available on the process are still those generated either directly or indirectly by the radicals,[132] the extent of Hua's real direct involvement in the process is probably far greater than that ascertainable from the body of materials available.

Hua Kuo-feng had assumed responsibility for the field of science and technology following the Fourth National People's Congress in January 1975.[133] That he continued to hold responsibility for this area throughout the year is indicated by his meetings with foreign scientific delegations: with a French telecommunications delegation on 27 June;

with science delegations from Pakistan on 23 July, Albania on 27 July, Denmark on 25 October, and Romania on 18 December; and with a French atomic energy delegation on 23 November.[134] In all probability, therefore, Hua played a key role in the drafting of the "Outline Report." This is indicated in qualitative terms in recent reporting,[135] but most of the details are lacking.

At some point in August Hua Kuo-feng convened a forum on science and technology. He "personally" invited scientific researchers from the Academy of Sciences to discuss a topic central to the "Outline Report"--i.e., how to pursue a policy of "letting a hundred flowers bloom and a hundred schools of thought contend" on the scientific and technological front. The participants are said to have put forward many good ideas and proposals. It is possible, depending upon the date that this meeting convened, that Hua conveyed to them the contents of the 1 August draft of the "Outline Report" and that their comments formed the basis for the revisions incorporated into the 17 August draft. Alternatively, this meeting may have taken place after the 17 August draft had been sent to Teng which then may partially explain the nine-day delay between Teng's receipt of this document and his decision to have Hu Ch'iao-mu revise it again. In either case, Hua Kuo-feng had the results of the forum edited and disseminated to lower levels by the Academy of Sciences.[136] He would not have done so had the "Outline Report" continued to run counter to the spirit of these remarks. Indeed, he could not have convened the forum in the first place on a topic of such central concern had he not been intimately involved in the drafting process itself, probably as the Politburo member directly in charge.[137] His dissemination of the forum's results even before the "Outline Report" had been adopted, moreover, suggests that he was trying to mobilize a constituency among scientists for this program.

By early September Hu Ch'iao-mu had revised the "Outline Report" draft in accordance with Teng's instructions. As per instructions, he took off some of the hard edges and added in a liberal sprinkling of quotations from Chairman Mao. Indeed, he virtually completely rewrote the second section of the draft so as to stress its explicit adherence to "Chairman Mao's revolutionary line on science and technology." To add still further to the political orthodoxy of the document, Hu appended to the draft a list of quotations on science and technology from revolutionary teachers throughout history.[138]

During September--again, the precise date is not available--the State Council convened a conference to consider this document. Hua

Kuo-feng, Teng Hsiao-p'ing, and Yeh Chien-ying, in their capacities as vice-premiers, participated in this meeting.[139] At its conclusion, this conference issued directives pertinent to the draft.[140]

The draft was then basically finalized, after repeated modifications and improvements, and on 26 September Teng Hsiao-p'ing convened a hui-pao meeting to discuss it.[141] This meeting was attended by Teng, Hu Ch'iao-mu, Hu Yao-pang, Li Ch'ang, Chou Jung-hsin, and possibly by others.[142] Hu Yao-pang first reported on the process of drafting the document and then on its contents. Teng interjected remarks at a number of points, and at the end he commented at length on many of the issues raised in the draft. Teng called for further revisions in certain parts of it, and he also told those assembled that they should not be afraid to act boldly in having the draft implemented--indeed, that they should try to whip up an outcry for the policies advocated in the draft. He advised them to focus future efforts on the critical problem of rectifying the leadership organs involved.

Concretely, Teng ordered that the draft be presented now to Mao Tse-tung for his comments, as "the Chairman is very concerned about this problem." He dictated that copies should then be made up and circulated to other members of the Politburo. He admonished his colleagues to act in the spirit of the Central Documents since Chung-fa #9 of that year,[143] and he also instructed Chou Jung-hsin to seize the initiative in the educational realm, as science and technology could not advance without appropriate changes in education.[144] This directive may well have provided the major spark for the events in the educational realm that came under public attack by the radicals in December 1975.[145]

The draft report was then given to Mao Tse-tung, who read it and gave instructions presenting his opinions.[146] A process of communicating the thrust of the draft and mobilizing support for it ensued. This process involved sending key cadres traveling around to lower levels; making speeches; drafting articles; writing letters; and planning the publication of a new journal that would reflect the viewpoint expressed in the "Outline Report." One leading cadre of the Academy of Sciences made a tour of the research institutes under the Academy, giving speeches, for instance, at the psychology and electronics institutes on 6 and 7 October; Hu Ch'iao-mu gave a talk on 6 October calling for publication of a new Party journal that would reflect the correct line; and so forth.[147]

To summarize briefly, the drafting process for the "Outline Summary Report on the Work of the Academy of Sciences" was highly consultative, involved substantial input from the professional people concerned, and evolved through a process of incremental adjustments as more information became available and as the political climate shifted. Mao Tse-tung, responding to a 1974 State Council report, provided the major impetus, which Teng quickly seized upon to start a concrete drafting process. The equivalent of a task force was created and sent to the Academy of Sciences to gather the information necessary and present a draft. There was repeated interaction between this task force and Teng Hsiao-p'ing's personal staff over the ensuing two and one-half months, with Hua Kuo-feng playing perhaps a key role in this process. At crucial stages the issue was put back on Teng Hsiao-p'ing's desk for his personal attention. Changes were made to accommodate a range of concerns: the views expressed by scientists in the Academy during the August forum convened by Hua; the opinions of leading members of the State Council including the head of the military, Yeh Chien-ying; and the need to put a better political gloss on the draft as a new political campaign--this one on the criticism of the Water Margin--got under way. Although Mao Tse-tung ostensibly initiated this process, the issue did not again cross the Chairman's desk until the end of September. It had remained largely bottled up within the science and technology system in the interim, as attested by the fact that, as noted above, Teng sent the final draft to Mao before having copies sent to the other members of the Politburo.

If this draft had Mao's backing and was being touted throughout the scientific circles, why did it suddenly become inoperative in the winter of 1975-76 until its resurrection in June 1977? The radicals tell us only that "when Chairman Mao personally initiated the struggle to beat back the right deviationist wind to reverse correct verdicts, they [i.e., the supporters of the "Outline Report"] were forced to withhold the final revised draft of the outline."[148] The actual situation was, in fact, more complicated than that, and a brief look at how the radicals stopped this policy document provides instructive insights about how the system worked as of late 1975.

The system of division of responsibility within the Politburo constrained the radicals and dictated their strategy for blocking the "Outline Report." Essentially, the Gang of Four lacked legitimate access to the document until it came up for consideration by the State Council where Chang Ch'un-ch'iao served as vice-premier. Fortunately for them, however, they had one of their political partisans in a responsible position in the Academy of Sciences and they worked through him to gain entree to the science and technology functional system.

Liu Chung-yang was deputy-secretary of the Academy of Sciences, one of the highest administrative positions in the Academy. He was also what is now termed a "follower of the Gang of Four."[149] Liu's position put him in the document stream for the Academy of Sciences, and he used this position to provide the Gang of Four with documents on the drafting of the "Outline Report" that otherwise they would not have been able to obtain. For this reason, the Chinese press have recently said that Liu (without naming him directly) "stole" the documents,[150] for the administrative rules concerning document flow clearly prohibited him from providing these items to someone outside of his functional system.

Before Liu performed his services, the radicals found that when the edited results of the August forum Hua Kuo-feng convened were circulated throughout the Academy of Sciences, their followers, who were evidently especially concentrated in one particular research institute, could only voice an "in house" criticism of the symposium and its results. These followers asserted that the symposium amounted to a "forum for airing complaints against the Great Cultural Revolution" and that it "slandered the excellent situation on the science and technology front." Consequently, the followers blocked the dissemination of the results of the forum wherever they could.[151]

As noted above, when Hu Yao-pang revised the initial draft in early August to take account of comments that had been made on it when it was circulated within the Academy, he failed to show this revised draft (i.e., the 17 August draft) to the Party core group in the Academy of Sciences before sending it to Hu Ch'iao-mu.[152] This omission may well have represented an attempt by Hu Yao-pang to keep Liu Chung-yang from learning the contents of the revised draft, as Liu probably belonged to the Party core group of the Academy. If so, subsequent events prove that Hu's caution was fully warranted.

When the State Council met during September, as noted above, Hua Kuo-feng, Teng Hsiao-p'ing, and Yeh Chien-ying made comments on the draft "Outline Report" and issued (probably oral) instructions. A stenographic record was kept of this meeting, as is the case with all such meetings in the PRC. Chang Ch'un-ch'iao, as the second-ranking vice-premier, very likely also attended this meeting, although no mention of his participation has been made in any source available to date. If he did participate, he probably became alarmed at what he heard, for the draft report implicitly or explicitly challenged the radicals' programs dealing with scientific research, policy toward intellectuals, and educational policy, among others. Chang, therefore, put pressure on his cohorts to utilize any means at their disposal to undermine this potentially dangerous effort.

The stenographic record of the State Council meeting was circulated within at least the highest levels of the Academy of Sciences. Liu Chung-yang made a copy of it and sent the copy to a follower of the Gang of Four at Tsinghua University, who in turn passed it on to one of the members of the radical faction in Shanghai. The Shanghai radicals then, purportedly acting on Chang Ch'un-ch'iao's direct orders, printed up several tens of thousands of copies of excerpts of the comments by Hua, Teng, and Yeh from these minutes and, without putting the name of the printer on the materials, distributed them to the basic levels in both Shanghai and other areas of the country "for use in criticism."[153] The Gang's "followers in Liaoning" (almost certainly referring to the Liaoning first secretary, Mao Tse-tung's nephew Mao Yuan-hsin) instructed their subordinates to criticize both the draft report and the remarks made by the three vice-premiers.[154]

At about the same time, Liu Chung-yang teamed up with his collaborator at Tsinghua University and collated a booklet of "reverse the verdicts" speeches and directives (including Central Documents).[155] These were documents that purportedly sought to change the "correct verdicts" of the Cultural Revolution across a wide range of issue areas. Almost certainly it was Liu who provided the texts of the speeches and directives pertinent to the science and technology system, to which his position would give him access. The Tsinghua contact contributed his skills in composition and reproduction. Liu Chung-yang then took this booklet and distributed it to the departments in Peking concerned with science and technology and to all twenty-nine provincial level administrative units.[156] Although the documentary evidence does not specify this, Liu probably sent the booklet only to departments at the provincial level <u>in the science and technology system</u>, as he lacked the bureaucratic power to give this booklet wider dissemination on his own authority. Alternatively, he may have distributed the booklet to partisans of the Gang of Four in each provincial level unit regardless of their spheres of responsibility.

At the same time that Liu was disseminating his booklet, Yao Wen-yuan issued a series of instructions that barred accurate press coverage of the "Outline Report" draft, and Yao told the reporters under him to keep a sharp eye out for stories that could be written on reversing the verdict in the sphere of science and technology.[157] The radicals, again probably relying on Liu Chung-yang's position, also organized a criticism meeting at the Academy of Sciences and sent reporters to give it full coverage. The meeting turned out to be a complete failure, however, and did not make the papers.[158]

Other events during the fall and winter of 1975-76 dramatically altered the political context in which this battle was waged. The Water Margin campaign of early fall evolved into a campaign against a reversal of verdicts in the sphere of education in November-December. Chou En-lai's death in January led to a severe internal battle that resulted in Hua Kuo-feng's appointment as acting premier in early February[159] and the launching of a campaign to criticize Teng Hsiao-p'ing. In this context, the February issue of Hung-ch'i carried an article sharply critical of the points made in the "Outline Report." Yao Wen-yuan purportedly commissioned this piece and provided the author with a copy of the booklet on the September 1975 State Council meeting to give him an accurate basis for his criticism.[160] During the confusing period from early February to early April, when Teng was down but not completely out, Liu Chung-yang wrote a piece saying that the "Outline Report" was in fact a modern variation of another famous outline report--the one that had been written by P'eng Chen in February 1966 and repudiated by Mao in May of that year.[161] This charge was then picked up and publicly aired by K'ang Li and Yen Feng in their "Study and Criticism" article in April that has been cited so often above.[162] The article by Liu Chung-yang in People's Daily followed afterward,[163] and the radicals purportedly wanted to launch a nationwide campaign focused on criticism of the "Outline Report." They could not, however, secure the agreement of the Central leadership (in which the central figure by that time was Hua Kuo-feng) for this campaign.[164]

In sum, the radicals lacked the executive power to block the drafting of the "Outline Report" in science and technology, as none of the highest ranking members of the radical group held responsibility for work in that sphere. They thus relied heavily on one of their followers in a leading position in the Academy of Sciences to provide them with information and documents,[165] and then they used their connections at Tsinghua University and in Shanghai and elsewhere to have these documents excerpted, reproduced and disseminated. Yao Wen-yuan used his own leverage in the media to try to create a furor about supposed attempts by "capitalist roaders" to reverse the verdict on the Cultural Revolution in the sphere of science and technology behind Mao's back. None of this, however, could really get underway until pertinent documents began to flow across Liu Chung-yang's desk at the Academy of

Sciences. The Gang of Four, moreover, found that they lacked allies or their own bureaucratic base to draft concrete alternative proposals for science and technology, and thus they were forced into a campaign of vilification and leaking of partial texts of documents in order to try to discredit the "Outline Report."

The available information does not make clear exactly when the "Outline Report" became inoperable.[166] Clearly, however, the above actions by the radicals amounted to no more than a delaying action, as the Gang of Four tried to find a lever that would really enable them to put a stop to the policy trends in this and related spheres that they perceived. They gradually forged this lever out of a combination of events in the fall of 1975 and winter of 1976, the details of which go beyond the scope of this paper. Suffice it to say that the "Outline Report" was too closely connected with Teng Hsiao-p'ing to long survive his overthrow--or to remain in limbo after his return to power. The June 1977 press coverage of the "Outline Report" makes clear that by then it had been adopted as official policy in the sphere of science and technology.

Certain Questions on Accelerating the Development of Industry (the "Twenty Articles"). There is far less information available on the drafting of this programmatic document for industry than is the case for the "Outline Report" concerning science and technology. Also, the available information on the drafting process for the "Twenty Articles" focuses almost exclusively on the roles of Teng Hsiao-p'ing in promoting the document and of the radicals in trying to undermine it. What is slighted is the major portion of the process that included the interaction of a functionally specialized member of the Politburo with the group that actually carried out the drafting, along with the modus operandi of this group. Still, the information available[167] does permit us to see the drafting process from Teng's vantage point. The outlines of this process emerge clearly from the available sources, and what these outlines portray conforms closely to the more detailed picture drawn above from the materials on the "Outline Report."

The year 1974 was a bad one for China's industry.[168] In response, Mao Tse-tung issued directives on pushing forward the national economy and on stability and unity, and in January 1975 the National People's Congress declared rapid achievement of the four modernizations to be national policy. This declaration was followed during the spring by Central Committee-sponsored conferences on two of the most critical problem areas--the railways and the iron and steel industry.[169] Central Documents on these respective problem areas were issued, and these in turn created the impetus for a more general set of principles, policies, and regulations that would govern and guide the entire field of industry. It was in this context that the authorities commissioned the drafting of "Certain Questions on Accelerating the Development of Industry."[170]

As noted above, we have available only the bare outline of the drafting process itself. This process began in July 1975, at roughly the same time as the start of the "Outline Report." A "leading comrade of the State Council" (almost certainly Teng Hsiao-p'ing) initiated the process. Standard practice would dictate that Teng hand this topic over to the person on the Politburo most concerned with the industrial sphere, who in turn would assign one of the executive organs in the system under him to carry out the actual drafting. The person on the Politburo responsible for industry would, by a process of elimination, have to be either Li Hsien-nien or Chi Teng-k'uei. Given their backgrounds, the odds in favor of Li are overwhelming, and I have assumed from here on that it was in fact Li who took control of the concrete drafting process. Li, in turn, handed the task over to the State Planning Commission under the leadership of Yü Ch'iu-li, as is indicated by a subsequent reference to a report from the State Planning Commission on this issue in September.[171]

Yü produced an initial fourteen-article draft for Teng's consideration by 17 August.[172] The fact that this draft was given to Teng on the same day as was the initial draft of the "Outline Report" strongly suggests that Teng had set this date as a deadline for both drafting efforts. He evidently spent the entire day reading and studying them. Teng had met with a foreign delegation on the day before but made no public appearance on 17 August. On the evening of 18 August he signed an economic and technical agreement with Cambodia and hosted a farewell banquet for the Cambodian delegation.[173] Given the foreign trade policy dimension of the "Outline Report" and the "Twenty Articles," the issues in the Sino-Cambodian negotiations meshed well with Teng's general concerns of those few days, although it is doubtful that the connection between these two programmatic documents and the Cambodian negotiation was very close. In any event, on 18 August Teng convened hui-pao meetings to discuss each of these drafts. The 18 August meeting on the "Outline Report" is analyzed in the preceding section. During the report meeting on the first draft of the "Twenty Articles," Teng Hsiao-p'ing stressed the need to emphasize rectification of the management of enterprises. He also repeatedly brought up the relationship of science and technology to industrial development and foreign trade--not a surprising theme in view of his other reading and activities during the previous twenty-four hours.[174]

Teng's comments sparked a process of repeated revisions of the draft. Altogether over the following three months this document underwent five substantial revisions and some thirty-two minor modifications. The first of these revisions was completed on 22 August. It added six articles to the original version, making now a total of twenty articles.[175] Given the fact that the available Ming Pao information concerning this document enumerates twenty articles and lacks the specific article on Party leadership that was a part of the next and all subsequent drafts, this must be the 22 August version of the "Twenty Articles."[176]

There is no specific record of Teng's having convened another hui-pao meeting on the 22 August draft, and it is possible that he never in fact commented directly on this version. This draft does contain a section on the rectification of enterprise management, although it was listed as the twelfth of the twenty articles. This draft also contains a section on adopting advanced technology (Article 10). Unfortunately, since no text of the fourteen-article draft of 17 August is available, it is not possible to determine whether or not these two articles were added on as a result of Teng's comments on 18 August. Two articles that are said to have been added specifically in response to Teng's comments at this meeting are those entitled "Increasing Exports of Industrial and Mineral Products" (Article 11) and "From Each According to His Ability, to Each According to His Work" (Article 16).[177]

Given the magnitude of the changes between this second draft (of 22 August) and the third draft that was submitted on 2 September, the drafters clearly did receive an important set of suggestions about the contents of this document from someone. Two logical possibilities suggest themselves, and they are not mutually exclusive. First, at some point during the drafting process this document was submitted to the heads ("responsible comrades") of twenty enterprises and to a meeting of the heads of twelve provincial Party committees that had convened in Peking. While no dates are given for these instances, it is possible that the comments from these two sets of reviewers in fact came back in late August.[178] The second possibility is that Li Hsien-nien convened his own hui-pao meeting on the subject and issued appropriate instructions.

The drafters of the 2 September text added sections on "Party Leadership" and "Relying on the Working Class" (Articles 2 and 3), dropped four articles, rewrote other articles, and changed the order of presentation of the articles carried over from the 22 August draft.[179] This version of the "Twenty Articles" thus actually contained eighteen articles. Overall, the changes in the draft seem to make this a document that is more clearly threatening to the radicals, as the substance and arrangement of this text put greater emphasis on the need to rectify Party committees and the management in enterprises than had the previous text.[180]

The radicals are said to have become particularly agitated over this version of the "Twenty Articles,"[181] and the presentation in the Kung Hsiao-wen article supports this contention. This agitation may, however, in fact indicate simply that they did not have access to any draft of this document prior to the 2 September draft.

That the radicals could not see any of the pre-September drafts is suggested by several considerations. First, the drafting process took place in the industry and communications and finance and trade systems, to which the radicals lacked direct access. Second, as noted above, the radicals mistakenly attribute the addition of the articles on wages and on increasing exports to the 2 September draft, when in fact they are included in the 22 August draft. The radicals based their allegation on the text they secured, containing Teng's remarks at the 18 August _hui-pao_ meeting. Thus, they probably never did see the 22 August draft, or that of 17 August, either. Third, in October Yao Wen-yuan claimed at a Politburo meeting that he had never seen a text of the "Twenty Articles." _People's Daily_ asserts in rebuttal, however, that Yao had in fact gained access to a text during _September_. This exercise in pinpointing the time at which the radicals obtained a detailed knowledge of the text of the "Twenty Articles" is significant in that it highlights once again the critical effects that the system of division of responsibility among Politburo members can have in structuring the maneuvering in Peking politics.

At some point during September, as noted above, the radicals learned of the contents of the 2 September draft and of the fact that either this or an earlier version of the document had already been circulated and had received a favorable response.[182] A somewhat different analysis from that given above would suggest that the presentation of the "Twenty Articles" to the meeting of twelve provincial Party heads and its circulation among twenty enterprises occurred in early September, and that the radicals learned of the draft's contents only through a partisan of theirs who either participated in the conference or was in the leadership of one of the enterprises. This construction of events gains credibility in view of the allegation that the text of the 2 September draft obtained by the radicals was handwritten and full of errors[183]--thus implying that it was copied illegally and quickly by someone who had temporary access to the draft as it circulated. Even this revised reconstruction of events, however, highlights the degree to which the division of responsibility and organization of functional systems in China channel information in politically important ways.

During the course of October, Teng Hsiao-p'ing seems to have tried to take some of the political rough edges off this draft in view of increasingly vocal opposition from the radicals. He thus turned the 2 September draft over to Hu Ch'iao-mu[184] for polishing. On 8 October the draft was modified in a small but important way. The reference to the "three directives as the key link"--a phrase that had earned the ire of the radicals by seemingly playing down the importance of class struggle--was replaced by the formulation "take the Party's basic line as the key link."[185] Hu then proceeded to recast the draft so as to make it politically more palatable in the atmosphere generated by the Water Margin campaign and the radicals' increasingly vociferous denunciations of those in China who retained a "comprador" philosophy. In this effort, while retaining the basic structure of the "Twenty Articles," Hu more than doubled the number of words in the text. Specifically, he added two articles (bringing the total back up to twenty): Article 1 on "Carrying Out Chairman Mao's Line on Developing Industry in an All-around Manner," which contained sixty-six quotations from the Chairman's works justifying the content of the draft; and Article 20 entitled "The Whole Party Should Get Mobilized to Fight for Accelerating the Speed of Industrial Development."[186] This draft was worked up and ready for presentation by 25 October.[187]

The State Planning Commission during October submitted a formal report to the Politburo that raised the question of the draft of the "Twenty Articles." The Commission's report recommended that after discussion by the Politburo the draft be submitted to a National Planning Conference for discussion. Yao Wen-yuan argued, however, that he felt the draft of the "Twenty Articles" was not yet "mature," that whether it could be presented at this time was therefore problematic, and that in view of this it would be best if the Planning Commission's report dropped all references to the "Twenty Articles."[188] Information in the Kung Hsiao-wen article suggests that this Politburo meeting may have occurred on or shortly before 25 October and indicates that the national conference to which the "Twenty Articles" was to be submitted was scheduled to meet at the end of October. Kung comments that the increasingly radicalized political atmosphere prevented the 25 October draft from again being revised and submitted to the conference.[189]

Indeed, the draft of the "Twenty Articles" seems to have been put aside for several months, until the radicals in early 1976 again used their network in Shanghai and at Peking and Tsinghua universities to print and distribute copies of the earlier drafts in an effort to blacken Teng Hsiao-p'ing. The radicals evidently continued this campaign of vilification right up until their overthrow in October. Aside from the media campaign and clandestine circulation of booklets of materials they had printed, this endeavor included a coordinated effort by the Shanghai and Liaoning participants in a July 1976 National Planning Work Symposium to obstruct serious consideration of the draft.[190] This would suggest that continuing attempts were made throughout 1976 to promulgate the "Twenty Articles," albeit without success, given the political turmoil of the period.

The above review demonstrates that the drafting process for the "Twenty Articles" shared roughly the same characteristics as those of the "Outline Report." Both, indeed, largely conform to the drafting process for major documents over the previous twenty-five years that was analyzed above. As embodied in the "Twenty Articles" drama, this is a process that involved an initial impulse from the top (albeit in response to pressing problems in the economy); a series of drafts generated by the bureaucracy that were circulated, commented upon, and revised; efforts in some of these revisions to make the language of the draft conform to the demands of a changing political atmosphere; and evidence of the channeling of information that results from the system of the Politburo division of responsibility and functional hierarchies which in turn keep a document largely bottled up within a given segment of the hierarchy until it is almost ready for final adoption. It is noteworthy, in this regard, that Yao Wen-yuan could not obtain legitimate access to a draft of the "Twenty Articles" until Li Hsien-nien and Teng Hsiao-p'ing brought it up to the Politburo for discussion via the Planning Commission report in October. Yao, however, had managed surreptitiously to obtain a handwritten copy of an earlier version in September, and he and his collaborators then used their control over the media (and their ability to leak information) in an attempt to block the adoption of this programmatic document. Thus, the different resources of each of the major sets of political actors, and the strategies that each accordingly adopted, emerge clearly from these two case studies of the drafting of particular documents during 1975. So, too, does the careful, incremental, and consultative administrative style of Teng Hsiao-p'ing emerge.

III. CENTRAL DOCUMENTS: THE TRANSMISSION PROCESS

Once a CD has been adopted and approved for dissemination, what is the procedure for transmitting (ch'uan-ta) it to the various units? Not surprisingly, considerable variation attends this process, depending on the contents of the document. Still, there are certain common elements that evidently apply to the transmission of virtually all CDs, regardless of the process by which they are drafted, how widely they are disseminated, their level of classification, the function they serve in the system, their rubric, and so forth. The following outline specifies these common dimensions of the process and indicates some of the types of variations that may be encountered as different documents flow through the system.

Many (perhaps most) Central Documents have a two-tiered transmission process: the first tier involves circulation of the actual document and is almost invariably intrabureaucratic; the second tier involves a wider dissemination of the contents of the CD--sometimes beyond the confines of the bureaucracy, often without the document itself being made available.

Every CD specifies concretely the units to which the document should be sent. Typically, this information appears as the first paragraph of the document. These units define the first tier of the transmission process. On almost all such documents available in the West, the units (called chu-sung chi-kuan in the vocabulary used concerning official documents in China) are both military and civilian[191] and encompass the Central down through the provincial (and sometimes hsien) level. Typical is the list of such organs for CD (72) #4 on the Lin Piao affair: "To the Party committees of each province, municipality (directly under the Central Government), and autonomous region; the Party committees of each military region, provincial military district, and field army; the Party committees of each general department of the Military Affairs Commission and each service branch; the leading groups and Party core groups of each department, ministry, and commission of the Central Committee and the State Council."[192] During the Cultural Revolution, CDs tended to be circulated more extensively, as this document stream was used to fulfill a wider range of communications functions. This wider dissemination is reflected, for instance, in the list of chu-sung chi-kuan for the CD on the "Suspension of the Big Exchange of Revolutionary Experience All over the Country" issued by the Central Committee on 19 March 1967: "To Party committees at all levels, Party committees of all military regions and districts, revolutionary committees of all provinces and municipalities, and all revolutionary mass organizations."[193] Note that this list not only includes organs down to the basic level but also encompasses non-Party as well as Party recipients.

In addition to the chu-sung chi-kuan detailed at the beginning of the CD, typically the last paragraph of the Central Document stipulates the groups to which the second tier of dissemination should be directed. To use the two CDs just cited, for example, the final paragraph of CD (72) #4 calls for transmission to be "divided into two steps: the first is to transmit it among the cadres, and the second, to the masses." The 19 March 1967 CD concluded with the instruction: "This circular may be posted in cities, the countryside and armed forces units."[194]

Central Documents are sent out to all organs on the chu-sung chi-kuan list simultaneously. When the Party General Office receives the CD at, for instance, the provincial level, the head of the General Office of the provincial Party committee sends the CD to the first secretary of the provincial Party committee, who in turn decides upon the process of further discussion and dissemination of the CD. If the document covers a relatively routine and functionally specialized subject, he may decide simply to consult with the Party secretary responsible for that area of work and, having decided on the best means of implementing the document, to send it down through channels from there. If the CD is of broader scope and greater importance, the first secretary will probably convene a meeting of the Standing Committee of the Party which will discuss how to transmit and implement the document. Almost certainly, the Party General Office would, under orders from the first secretary, have made enough copies of the document for each of the members of the Standing Committee to use for reference. The Standing Committee would most likely stipulate the forms to be used in the further dissemination process, perhaps under some guidance from Peking, and write its own covering document expressing its opinions on the implementation of the CD in the area under its jurisdiction.

The Standing Committee can then convene a meeting of the entire Party committee, of key cadres from the department under the Party committee or from several levels down the hierarchy, or of any other group appropriate for purposes of transmitting the contents of the document. Alternatively, it can eschew a meeting process entirely and rely instead strictly on written communications passed along the appropriate bureaucratic channels. Thus, the actual process of transmission of a document varies according to the needs of the moment, and the entire process typically is geared to achieving the most effective implementation of the demands of the CD without violating the instructions of the Center and the possibilities afforded by local conditions.

When the Standing Committee receives a document that its members feel warrants dissemination via a meeting format, then "transmission meetings" (ch'uan-ta hui-i) in relevant units are convened.[195] At these, the responsible person (usually the first secretary of the unit) announces that "CD (year) (no.)" has just been received. He then either reads or summarizes the text of the document to the meeting. The rules on note taking vary and are specified at the beginning of the meeting. At the end of the secretary's recitation, he may proceed to call attention to some particular points that are regarded as the central elements in the document or provide some other explanatory information. He then calls for questions, which at this point usually are limited to requests that he repeat some part of what he had said because the person could not hear or understand it all. This type of request occurs quite frequently and is always honored.[196]

Sometimes the people attending this ch'uan-ta meeting break up into small groups to review the document item by item and gain a clearer and more detailed understanding of both the contents of the CD and the way the material should be handled. In these small groups the participants can raise detailed questions about the material--questions that will be referred to higher levels if necessary. The range of questioning, however, will be dictated in part by the rubric on the CD as discussed above.

Thus, the first tier transmission of the CD typically involves key personnel and consists of a relatively full rendition of the contents of the document, efforts to unify thinking on the issues concerned, and concrete preparations for wider dissemination. The first tier transmission of CD (72) #4 illustrates this dimension of the ch'uan-ta process. This Central Document circulated the "second batch" of materials on the "Lin Piao--Ch'en Po-ta anti-Party clique." The "second batch" included prominently the famous "571" document, Lin Piao's purported plan (drafted by Lin Li-kuo and his colleagues) for an armed coup d'etat against Mao Tse-tung.[197]

The Lin Piao affair presented the Central leadership with one of its greatest challenges since 1949. Mao had personally annointed Lin his heir apparent, and the traumatic Cultural Revolution had been widely seen as issuing from the political alliance of the Party Chairman and his head of the armed forces. Thus, Lin's dramatic demise in a plane crash while reportedly fleeing to the Soviet Union after an assassination attempt against Mao Tse-tung sent shock waves throughout the Party and the country. The task of explaining this event to Party officials throughout the bureaucracy as well as to the masses posed a major problem, and CD (72) #4 conveyed one of the key sets of documents concerning this affair. Clearly, this was a CD that had to be handled with more than the usual amount of care given to the process of transmission, for the issues involved were potentially explosive and cynicism toward the explanations given was likely to be widespread.[198] Not surprisingly, then, this document spread through a somewhat more elaborate transmission process than was typical, but the basic outlines remained the same as those sketched above.

The <u>chu-sung chi-kuan</u> listed for CD (72) #4, as previously noted, included the Party committees of both the provinces and the military regions. Since in Yunnan the seats of both of these are in Kunming, the leadership at this level decided to transmit the CD via a joint meeting of cadres of both the Yunnan Provincial Party Committee and the Party Committee of the Kunming Military Region. Our information about the <u>ch'uan-ta</u> process for this document comes almost exclusively from the available text of the summation speech given at this joint meeting by Wang Pi-ch'eng, who at that time concurrently served as commander of the Kunming Military Region, second secretary of the Yunnan Party Committee, and first vice-chairman of the Yunnan Provincial Revolutionary Committee.[199] The <u>ch'uan-ta</u> meeting itself assumed a format resembling that of a work conference, with an initial plenary session, followed by a number of days of small group discussion of the issues concerned, and capped by a final plenary session and summary report. The entire meeting lasted ten days and involved 1, 851 participants, of whom 841 were from the military system and 1, 010 hailed from the civilian sector.[200]

CD (72) #4 was issued by the Central authorities on 13 January, and the Yunnan transmission meeting convened from 28 January to

6 February. Thus, it took half a month before this document was presented by the provincial leadership to the provincial level cadres specified in the chu-sung chi-kuan list. This delay in transmission is not very much out of the ordinary, except that in this case the document was of such high priority that one would normally have anticipated more rapid dissemination. The pause seems to be accounted for by the fact that the Central leadership took the precaution of first disseminating the document in key points to test the reaction it would cause--the kinds of questions raised and how best to deal with them. Indeed, this key point transmission went all the way down to the grass roots level before the document was more widely distributed among the Party cadres throughout the country[201]--an indication of the extraordinary concern Peking displayed over the possible reactions to the revelations contained in this material. Having analyzed the response this document engendered at the key points, the leadership felt confident enough to disseminate it more widely within the Party--certainly with appropriate directions to the leading personnel at each level on what questions they should anticipate and how they should handle them. The CD itself also provided some guidance on what should be stressed in the study of the accompanying reference materials.

The provincial level transmission meeting in Yunnan began with an address by Chou Hsing, a vice-chairman of the Yunnan Revolutionary Committee and political commissar of the Kunming Military Region.[202] Chou first read verbatim the text of CD (72) #4 and the appended materials to the audience assembled and then criticized the contents of the "571" documents, thereby indicating the way this extraordinarily sensitive revelation of a coup plan should be handled. The meeting then broke up into separate study groups, and over the following eight days the participants attended both these groups and one or more plenary sessions. In the small groups, these participants criticized the materials provided on Lin Piao's plans "line by line" and studied what these materials revealed about Lin's real character, motives, and politics.[203] They were also provided with appropriate materials from Lin's public utterances in recent years so as to highlight the contrast between what he said in public and what he actually felt as revealed in the reference materials circulated with the CD (thus proving what a "double-dealer" Lin actually was).[204] People were encouraged to express their views during the study groups, and a number of them took advantage of this opportunity to indicate that they had misgivings either about the materials circulated by CD (72) #4 or about presenting these materials to a wider audience later on.[205] The plenary session(s) presumably summed up the discussions to each point, specified the key problem areas, and provided some guidance to put the small group discussions back on a smooth track. During this small group study period, the various participants also developed concrete plans for disseminating the document to wider audiences--including eventually the general public--as had been called for in the second tier dissemination instructions in the CD. These plans stipulated a process, in the following order, of: transmitting the document in key test points in order to gain experience; having the cadres study the document well so that they could deal with all problems that might arise; cultivating "backbone" personnel to help lead the discussion of the document; and developing a clear plan as to how to direct each phase of the masses' study of the document. Only when all these preparations had been made would the masses be told the contents of CD (72) #4.[206]

Wang Pi-ch'eng summed up the work of this meeting at a plenary session on the final day of the convocation. His speech, which was classified "chüeh-mi" (absolutely secret), reviewed the progress of the transmission meeting, recounted some of the problems that had been encountered, laid out in no uncertain terms the "correct" attitude to take toward the range of issues that had been raised both by the Central Document itself and by the discussions over the preceding days, provided a pep talk to those who still held doubts about what the public response to CD (72) #4 would be, and laid out in broad brush the plans for further dissemination of the document. This last item in Wang's speech shifts our attention to the second tier of dissemination of a CD and the problems involved in making the contents of a CD known to a wider audience.

The second tier dissemination of a CD varies extremely widely in the techniques used and the time period involved. In part, it involves further transmission of the document within the bureaucracies--to lower ranking cadres, general Party members, and non-Party civil servants. For some documents, such as CD (72) #4, there is further dissemination to the general public. What is actually circulated at these levels typically is not the original document but rather a copy of it made by one of the chu-sung chi-kuan,[207] which sometimes excludes the CD covering letter and conveys only the reference materials originally attached as appendices. The different techniques employed make it worth tracing this second tier dissemination separately in its intra- and extra-bureaucratic dimensions.

A CD is usually sent simultaneously to all bureaucratic units involved in the second tier transmission. Sometimes, communicating the contents of the CD can take the form of convening a multilevel cadre meeting for relevant personnel from the second tier units, who will then return to their individual units to report on what they have been told. At other times, a copy of the CD itself is sent to the second tier units, along with a covering document from the chu-sung chi-kuan that indicates any opinions that organ has on the issues concerned. A third method entails sending out cadres from the chu-sung chi-kuan to the second tier units to instruct them on the contents of the CD and how to handle it. For instance, as part of the process of transmitting CD (74) #21 on the need to "grasp revolution and promote production" in the campaign to criticize Lin Piao and Confucius, the Kiangsi Provincial Party Committee convened a meeting of leading members of the provincial departments. The Committee then dispatched these leading cadres to the rural and industrial and mining areas to help units in these places implement the CD.[208]

A telephone conference is another frequently used vehicle for transmitting the contents of a document from one level to the leadership cadres of the next lower level. This type of conference is probably of particular value in large provinces and in the rural areas. On 8 July 1974, for instance, Szechwan's Provincial Party Committee convened a telephone conference to transmit the contents of CD (74) #21. This conference linked together the leading Party cadres of all regional, municipal, autonomous chou and county committees and provincial departments. Li Ta-chang, secretary of the provincial Party committee, spoke at the conference and transmitted the basic contents of CD (74) #21.[209] Other provinces using telephone conferences to transmit this directive included Yunnan,[210] Kiangsu,[211] Honan,[212] and Heilungkiang.[213] In sum, the forms used for dissemination can vary widely. Not infrequently, moreover, only the summary of a CD, not the CD itself, is circulated in the second tier units.

When ch'uan-ta meetings have been ordered as a part of the process of intrabureaucratic second tier dissemination of a CD, the format of these meetings seems to follow closely that used in their counterparts in the first tier organs. One non-Party informant described a part of this process thus:

> Following the [second tier] ch'uan-ta meeting, the participants usually break up into their usual study groups. The person leading each study group has been briefed in advance on the contents of the document and has been given advice on how to handle the discussion of it. Often, he begins the study group by again reading the document or its summary to the participants. The document itself,

however, is not circulated for their perusal, as every effort is made to keep the number of original copies down to a minimum and exercise tight control over their dissemination.[214] The study group leader entertains requests for yet another reading of portions that remain unclear, and then he leads discussion of the contents of the document. This discussion of contents can be very detailed or rather pro forma, depending on how directly relevant the document is to the particular unit concerned. Indeed, for some CDs that are considered not very important for the receiving unit, the leadership can disregard the _ch'uan-ta hui-i_ and utilize only the study group format for introducing and discussing the document. For others more directly pertinent, the _ch'uan-ta_ process may include serious discussion of the means to implement the Central decision.

Any person under a political cloud is excluded even from the transmission of the document to the non-Party people in the unit. This exclusion automatically applies to the five bad elements, and it is usually also applied to anyone who is currently under suspicion even if the person himself is not yet aware that he is in political difficulty. Other types of exclusions can also come into play. For instance, it is not very rare for a document to be transmitted only to those non-Party cadres above a particular civil service rank or to those who specialize in the areas with which the CD is concerned. Thus, if a cadre knows that a CD has been transmitted in his unit and he has not been invited to participate, it behooves him to find out what the subject of the document is. If it concerns a general political issue (such as the purge of Lin Piao), the cadre might take his exclusion from the _ch'uan-ta_ process as a fairly firm indication that he is under investigation for some offense.

The sphere for second tier transmission of a CD is, as mentioned above, determined by the leadership in the pertinent first tier organ in conformity with instructions from the Center and the contents of the document. Clearly political issues evidently receive wider dissemination, as there is no functional demarcation inherent in the subject matter that excludes a particular portion of the people. Naturally, some of the "political" CDs may concern issues so sensitive that they remain tightly held within the Party bureaucracy. The more functionally oriented CDs are evidently more likely to be transmitted only to those whose jobs make it desirable for them to be briefed on the contents of the CD.

Wang Pi-ch'eng's summary speech again provides underpinning for some of the above generalizations, which were derived primarily from interviewing. Wang, for instance, stresses the need to have the cadres and discussion leaders fully understand the CD before it is more broadly communicated.[215] He also notes that further transmission will bring the CD to the attention of everyone in China except the five bad elements.[216] Thus, the transmission of Central Documents in the PRC proceeds level by level (i.e., from the top down) and from the inside to the outside (i.e., from the Party core to non-Party bureaucrats and then to the public), with the leaders stipulating a cutoff at any point they deem appropriate. The political outcasts of society are evidently always felt to be beyond the pale in the ch'uan-ta process.

Once one goes "beyond" the strictly intrabureaucratic sphere and looks at how the substance of a CD is transmitted to the masses, the variety of techniques encountered becomes extraordinarily rich. The common people may be brought into the ch'uan-ta process via listening to appropriate speeches on radio or television, reading editorials and feature articles in the newspapers, attending a special rally or a meeting of the mass organization to which they belong, or learning the contents of a document through a meeting of their regular study group.[217] A person may also become aware of a document through being invited to participate in an endeavor that grows out of a Central Document, as was the case for people who participated in the National Agricultural Science and Technology Conference of February-March 1963. The twelve hundred scientists who attended had clearly been drawn into work mandated by the Tenth Plenum of the Eighth Central Committee the previous September.[218] The one common feature among dissemination techniques is that only rarely are the contents of an entire CD communicated verbatim to the public. Again let us turn to a case study--this time a detailed review of the transmission process for CD (74) #21--to highlight some important aspects of the process of transmitting the contents of a CD to the public.

As noted above, CD (74) #21 was issued on 1 July 1974. This was at a time when the campaign to criticize Lin Piao and Confucius had peaked and caused widespread disruption, which in turn was paralyzing sections of the economy. While affirming the correctness of the campaign and the value of this experience, therefore, the CD focused particularly on the need to "grasp revolution and promote production," leaving no doubt that it was the latter part of this well-known slogan that should be the touchstone of policy in the current period. In somewhat more detail, the contents of this CD's ten articles are as follows:[219] Article 1 praises the current situation and asserts that industrial and agricultural production will continue to improve as the campaign to criticize Lin Piao and Confucius is continued and deepened; Article 2 calls for "serious attention" to be devoted to shortfalls in coal and steel production and in rail transport, with the major offending locales stipulated in the text; Article 3 attributes a part of these problems to deviations in carrying out the p'i-Lin p'i-K'ung (PLPK) campaign, asserting that these have allowed "a small handful of class enemies to take the opportunity to bring up the surges, engage in destruction and disrupt order"; Article 4 focuses on Mao's evaluation that "the great majority of cadres are good" and calls for policies to allow cadres who have made mistakes to rectify them and to be again on good terms with the masses; Article 5 articulates a series of measures for dealing with the problem of cadres who have ceased coming to the office because they are under fire; Article 6 condemns "economism" and stipulates that questions about wages that have arisen are to be put off until the latter stage of the campaign; Article 7 stresses that "going against the tide" must be carried out based on a class analysis and condemns those who engage in mountain strongholdism and factionalism; Article 8 calls for the leadership to suppress people who disturb social order and commit economic crimes; Article 9 calls on all Party and Youth League members to help propagate the experiences of those who successfully integrate p'i-Lin p'i-K'ung with promoting production; and Article 10 directs the Party committees at various levels to review the situation and effectively mesh the campaign against Lin and Confucius with fulfillment of the various economic plans of the state.

Overall, then, this document touches on a wide range of dimensions of the problem of increasing production, instilling discipline and maintaining public order while continuing to carry out the campaign to criticize Lin Piao and Confucius. It calls for continuing attention to the campaign but makes clear, as happened in the Cultural Revolution and previous political movements, that the campaign's goals had in fact changed--in this case, that the campaign must now serve the cause of increasing production. This multifaceted document was one of the most important CDs issued during 1974. It bore the rubric t'ung-chih, thus indicating (not surprisingly, given the tremendous variations in local conditions around the country) that the Central authorities expected local leaders to act in accordance with the spirit (ching-shen) rather than the letter of this document. The first tier dissemination of this document was stipulated down to the provincial level[220] with second tier dissemination required to the counties[221] and then to the general public. In some provinces, second tier dissemination commenced as early as 5 July, while in other provinces there is no visible evidence of this level of dissemination until as late as early August. Fourteen of the nineteen provinces on which such data are available, however, commenced second tier dissemination by 15 July.[222]

Not surprisingly, there is no geographical pattern that explains the sequence of second tier dissemination for CD (74) #21. Distant Yunnan commenced this process within five days of the issuance of the CD, while nearby Shantung did not show evidence of engaging in this work until almost four weeks later. The overall rapidity of dissemination is noteworthy, however, and seems to have resulted from two factors. First, the document was considered top priority and therefore received urgent treatment. Second, the document was sufficiently broad in scope, with specific references to economic conditions in various units and a wide range of concrete policy prescriptions, that the drafting process for it must have involved quite a few provincial and subprovincial level bodies. The lower levels were, therefore, probably well aware of the general thrust and contents of the document in advance of its formal adoption and issuance,[223] and this familiarity may in turn have facilitated the process of dissemination.

The level-by-level and inside-to-outside approach to second tier dissemination of the contents of CD (74) #21 emerges clearly from the local media reports of July-August 1974, as illustrated by the following examples from individual provinces. The Yunnan Provincial Party Committee convened a telephone conference for Party cadres on 5 July. Four days later the provincial and Kunming municipal Trade Union Federation, Women's Federation, and Youth League sponsored a "pledge rally" attended by workers, poor and lower middle peasants, and the staff and workers of the finance and trade front in the city to convey the contents of CD #21.[224] Szechwan province began its second tier dissemination process with the 8 July intrabureaucratic telephone conference mentioned above. This conference linked up the leading Party cadres at the provincial level with those in the prefectural, municipal, autonomous chou and hsien Party committees. Seven days later the provincial Party committee convened a ten-day provincial conference on grasping revolution and promoting production in industry and communications attended by some 1,700 cadres and regular employees from that functional system. The purpose of this conference was to transmit and discuss how to implement the contents of CD (74) #21.[225] On 18 July the Szechwan provincial and Ch'engtu municipal federations of trade unions held a joint "oath taking rally" attended by 13,700 workers from the industry, communications, and finance and trade fronts at which the leaders transmitted the contents of CD (74) #21 to this large audience.[226] Finally, on 22 July, the Szechwan Daily published an editorial that transmitted the basic contents of CD (74) #21. Indeed, this editorial quoted extensively from several articles of the CD, albeit without mentioning that these were direct quotations.[227] In Kiangsu, likewise, the second tier dissemination began with a telephone conference convened by the provincial Party committee on 8 July which transmitted CD (74) #21 to responsible cadres at the provincial, prefectural, municipal and county levels in the Party, government and mass organizations.[228] Two days later in Nanking the municipal Party committee convened a rally of 50,000 representatives of the cadres and masses at Wutaishan Stadium to transmit the message of the CD. A rash of other meetings was held in the municipality on the same day to exchange experiences relevant to grasping revolution and promoting production, to take oaths to carry out the spirit of CD #21, and to commend model units who exemplified the virtues called for in the Central Document.[229] On 15 August, Kiangsu Radio carried an editorial from the province's Hsinhua Daily entitled "Uphold the Great Principle of Grasping Revolution and Promoting Production." This editorial also conveyed the contents of CD (74) #21.[230] In each of these instances, then, second tier dissemination went from provincial level to lower level to the general public and, on the whole, from Party cadres to non-Party cadres to ordinary citizens.

Among the plethora of groups that met to hear the contents of CD (74) #21, one type that appears repeatedly in different provinces is meetings of the functional systems for which the Central Document is particularly pertinent. Kweichow, for instance, convened a special conference on finance and trade for 10-22 August;[231] Shantung held a telephone conference on grasping revolution and promoting production in the province's coal industry on 16 August;[232] Kiangsi also convened a province-wide conference on the coal industry[233] as well as a related meeting on the metallurgical industry,[234] while Kirin convened an eight-day conference of personnel from the industrial and communications system.[235] Hupeh held a conference of Party secretaries responsible for industry,[236] and Szechwan convened the above-mentioned conference of people from the industry and communications system.[237] Another frequently seen meeting was that convened by the trade union organizations, which in mid-1974 were just recently reconstructed after having been virtually destroyed during the Cultural Revolution. A significant component of CD (74) #21 focused on matters of primary concern to workers--factory discipline, production quotas, and wages. Thus, it is wholly appropriate that the newly reorganized trade unions should have been called on to play a major role in communicating the contents of this CD to the workers in various enterprises. Ch'uan-ta meetings and rallies either sponsored or cosponsored by the trade union organizations were reported in Kiangsu,[238] Kweichow,[239] Szechwan,[240] and Yunnan[241] provinces. A common dimension of the second tier dissemination process, then, is to convene meetings of functionally defined groups of people who are directly concerned with the message of the Central Document.

Other devices that were mentioned in the media (excluding the articles and editorials in the papers themselves) for communicating CD (74) #21 to the public included the following: oath-taking rallies,[242] regional broadcast rallies,[243] pledge rallies,[244] mobilization rallies,[245] and symposia to exchange experiences,[246] in addition to the various specialized meetings and conferences mentioned above.

The media reports on these events seem to indicate that the leadership conveyed only parts of CD (74) #21 to the public via these forums. Naturally, these seeming omissions may in fact reflect selective reporting of the events rather than the events themselves. Similarly, somewhat fuller versions of the document may have been transmitted via the study group network than were conveyed in the more ostentatious public gatherings (although one knowledgeable informant doubted that this would in fact be the case). It is striking, in this connection, to find that local editorials written to convey the contents of the CD exhibited similar selectivity,[247] suggesting that this derived from a conscious policy of limiting the public dissemination of sections of the document. Thus, it appears from the media materials available that provincial political leaders conveyed only a part of the contents of the document to many people in the second tier of dissemination in their provinces. Indeed, in several instances there is evidence that provincial (in both senses of the word) considerations skewed the transmission process in various locales and the ways in which this was done. This may well have reflected a conscious strategy of taking political advantage of the complexity of the ten articles in CD (74) #21 and the flexibility generally allowed by the use of a t'ung-chih rubric.

Some local leaders simply conveyed a significantly different thrust on key issues from that contained in the CD--all in the name of transmitting the contents of the CD. For example, Article 8 of CD #21 states that "we must sufficiently (ch'ung-fen) mobilize the masses, make the dictatorial organs function properly and resolutely attack those enemies who undermine the criticism of Lin Piao and Confucius, undermine the industrial and agricultural production, and undermine the communications and transportation." In short, the thrust of this article (and of the entire document) is to crack down on disruption so as to reestablish order, stop struggle, and increase production. The official summary of the 8 July Szechwan telephone conference that linked the provincial Party committee up with the leading cadres of the provincial departments and of the prefectural, hsien, municipal and autonomous chou Party committees in order to transmit CD#21, by contrast, argued that "we must trust and rely on the masses and give them free rein . . . ,"[248] which goes directly against the spirit of the Central Document although it plays off of the CD's acknowledgement that one should continue to mobilize the masses "sufficiently." Indeed, this entire Szechwan telephone conference as reported in the media took on a distinctly different aura from that of the CD it was convened to transmit. For example, CD#21 begins with a brief review of the situation to date, which notes that "the campaign to criticize Lin Piao and Confucius has already been carried out in the cities and villages throughout the country and is developing deeply, universally, and persistently. The masses of people have been mobilized."[249] The remainder of the document, as noted previously, downplays the p'i-Lin p'i-K'ung campaign and in fact completely restructures the goals of the campaign toward order, discipline, and production. The Szechwan telephone conference, by contrast, stressed that "the most fundamental thing is to grasp the line. At present, this means carrying out criticism of Lin and Confucius deeply, universally and protractedly."[250] The original Chinese Central Document was clear in its use of the past tense on the mobilization phase of the p'i-Lin p'i-K'ung campaign--and the conference was equally clear[251] on shifting it to the present tense and making it the key focus of current policy. The conference summary argues further that the Szechwan leadership should "embrace still more firmly the idea of fighting a protracted war and strengthen spontaneity. . . . We must resolutely support the masses' proletarian revolutionary spirit and welcome their criticism and supervision. We should plunge among the masses, sum up experiences in mass struggle [which presumes--contrary to the message of the CD--that "struggle" should continue], concentrate them and persist in them."[252] Thus, although this broadcast on the telephone conference also includes substantial terminology that is found verbatim in the CD, the policies stipulated by the conference, if accurately reported on Szechwan Radio and translated in FBIS/PRC, considerably shifted the balance between the tasks of revolution and of production from that dictated in CD#21.

Chekiang province's dissemination of CD (74)#21 provides an even more striking example of an attempt to refocus the thrust of this important Central Document. CD #21 had been issued on 1 July, and the provincial leadership clearly had the document in hand within a day or two, as indicated by the fact that second tier dissemination had begun in Yunnan as early as 5 July.[253] Nevertheless, on 5 July a meeting was convened in the name of the Chekiang Provincial Party Committee and presided over by Weng Sen-ho, who has subsequently been denounced as one of the key followers of the Gang of Four. This mass meeting, attended by many high-ranking officials, was convened in the name of pushing forward the campaign to criticize Lin and Confucius and devoted most of its attention to the major themes of that campaign--criticizing those who want to "restrain oneself and restore the rights," denouncing those who would seek to become the head of state, and so forth. The meeting concluded that "it is necessary to continuously criticize the rightist trend which advocates retrogression and restoration, and negates the Great Proletarian Cultural Revolution and socialist new things."[254]

This same meeting called on cadres (almost as an afterthought, if the broadcasted review of the meeting accurately reflects the proceedings) to grasp production and map out effective measures for increasing production. It then closely paraphrased CD #21 in stating that the cadres "must fully mobilize the masses to resolutely strike at class enemies who are trying to sabotage the movement to criticize Lin Piao and Confucius."[255] This admonition differs in two crucial respects, however, from the actual decision expressed in Article 8 of CD #21. First, Article 8 clearly states that both the mobilized masses <u>and the dictatorial organs of the state</u> should be brought into play to suppress the class enemies, while the Chekiang meeting entrusted this task solely to the "mobilized masses." Secondly, Article 8 called for suppression of those who oppose the PLPK campaign and of those who disrupt either industrial and agricultural production or communications and transportation. Weng Sen-ho's meeting omitted the latter two dimensions of this important stricture. By transmitting only a part of the text of Article 8, then, this meeting seriously distorted the meaning of the document the provincial leadership had just been told to disseminate.

Weng Sen-ho's meeting utilized another device that was also employed by other provincial leaders in transmitting this document--to wit, the meeting called on its participants to "further implement the <u>series of</u> important directives of Chairman Mao and the Central Committee. . . ."[256] Earlier CDs evidently had been more to the liking of the radicals, and CD #21 did not explicitly negate earlier Central Documents. Rather, it turned around the thrust of the PLPK campaign simply by specifying the key current problems and tasks in a way that differed from earlier analyses. By meshing CD #21 with the earlier CDs on PLPK, therefore, provincial leaders could dilute somewhat the parts of CD #21 that they found objectionable.[257] The fact that during 1974 the provincial leaders were receiving a new CD virtually every ten days must have made this an attractive ploy to use in the transmission process.[258]

Thus, Weng Sen-ho and his colleagues in the Chekiang provincial leadership distorted CD #21 in the process of transmitting this document. Specifically, they focused on PLPK instead of on increasing production and upholding discipline. They quoted from one of the major articles of the CD, but omitted a key passage on the use of "dictatorial organs" and left out two of the three objects of exercising this dictatorship. Finally, they "packaged" CD #21 by meshing it with a whole series of CDs on the PLPK campaign, thus mitigating some of the force of this individual document. Not surprisingly, Weng Sen-ho came under fire as a member of the radical faction soon after the October 1976 purge of the Gang of Four.

A meeting of the key military, Party and government leaders in Hunan province that convened toward the middle of July[259] used many of the same tactics to distort the thrust of CD (74) #21 in the province. This meeting, for instance, convened "with a view to implementing the series of important instructions of Chairman Mao and the Party Center on criticizing Lin and Confucius and on various other work" [emphasis added]. The meeting then focused almost all its attention on overcoming the obstacles that had been encountered in fully carrying out the PLPK campaign in the province, giving barely a nod to the production issues brought up in CD #21. Since CD #21 was clearly on the agenda, though, the provincial leadership could not wholly ignore consideration of the task of increasing production. Rather, it called for an all-out effort to "propagate and implement on a grand scale the instructions of the Center on grasping revolution and promoting production." To implement this, it directed that "while devoting their main efforts to leading the campaign, the CCP committees must also strengthen their leadership over production"--a distribution of effort sharply at variance with the thrust of CD #21. This meeting thus managed to keep its focus on mobilization, struggle, and battles to prevent a reversal of verdicts on the Cultural Revolution and the socialist newborn things while also formally transmitting and studying CD #21.

Another critical dimension of the transmission process for Central Documents is highlighted by some additional "distortions" of CD (74) #21 in this Hunan meeting. In the name of uniting the cadres of the Party committees, this meeting called operationally for "unfolding within the CCP committees struggle between the correct and incorrect lines and struggle between correct and incorrect ideas." While quoting from Article 4 of CD#21 to the effect that "the great majority of cadres are good. . . . In compliance with the principle 'learn past mistakes to avoid future ones and cure the sickness to save the patient,' we must take a correct attitude to erring comrades," it inserted between these quoted sentences a sentiment not found in CD#21--i. e., "the masses must exercise revolutionary supervision over leadership cadres and vigorously support their work."

Where did these discordant ideas originate? The answer, in this case, is clear: from the People's Daily editorial published on the same day that CD(74)#21 was distributed! This 1 July editorial[260] did not launch a frontal attack on its Central Document counterpart. Rather, it partly complemented the message in the CD (that the Party committees must assume firm leadership over the PLPK campaign); partly ignored it (by, for instance, mentioning "grasp revolution, promote production" only in the final line, and even then merely as a slogan without specific content); and partly undermined it (by calling for struggle as the means to attain unity in the Party committees and stressing the mobilization of the masses and their supervision over the leadership). In mid-1974 provincial leaders around the country and their subordinates thus received two highly authoritative communications from Peking with identical dates. Both were very important (a wide-ranging Central Document articulating a new policy line on a current political movement and the annual 1 July editorial in honor of the founding of the Party), and yet the spirit of each differed enough to allow lower level leaders to modify the message of either by adjusting the mix between them in the dissemination process. Some provincial cadres, such as those that convened the mid-July transmission meeting in Hunan province, clearly took advantage of the latitude afforded by this situation.

Had People's Daily editorials traditionally had an adversary relationship with internal Central Committee communications? Clearly not. Before the Cultural Revolution, indeed, major Central Documents as a matter of course generated one or more People's Daily editorials that amplified the points in either a part or the entirety of the document. Some of these editorials were published weeks or months after the dissemination of the Central Document so as to provide guidance on problems that had arisen in the process of implementation. Since People's Daily editorials are required subjects for study in most of the study groups in China, then, they were used by the Central leadership as an efficient means to amplify policies communicated in CDs to lower level cadres and the public. This is not meant to imply that all, or even a majority, of pre-1966 People's Daily editorials communicated the contents of Central Documents. It also should not be construed as indicating that all CDs generated their own People's Daily editorials. Rather, it simply indicates that an important and wide-ranging CD would very likely serve as the source for one or more JMJP editorials during the weeks and perhaps months following its dissemination by the Central authorities.

A brief look at the use of JMJP editorials to communicate the contents of the series of major Central Documents on the Socialist Education Campaign during 1963-65 illustrates the basic points about this editorial practice. Four important CDs initiated and then molded the contours of this campaign: the "Former Ten Points," the "Later Ten Points," the "Revised Later Ten Points," and the "Twenty-three Points."[261] Mao Tse-tung authored the first and last of these, while Teng Hsiao-p'ing and Liu Shao-ch'i are said to have been responsible for the other two. This campaign was, moreover, a subject of intense debate in China during this period.[262] The discussion of the contents of these documents in JMJP editorials (without ever explicitly mentioning a CD itself) was as follows:

Editorial Date	Document	Article Number Reflected in Editorial
29 May 1963	"Former Ten Points"	6
2 June 1963	"	9
4 July 1963	"	9
17 July 1963	"	9
21 July 1963	"	9
29 July 1963	"	9
17 August 1963	"	9
29 November 1963	"Later Ten Points"	1
7 December 1963	"	1
1 January 1964	"	Introduction
19 March 1964	"	1
24 March 1964	"	1
26 March 1964	"	1
28 August 1964	"	7
30 August 1964	"	7
17 November 1964	"Revised Later Ten Points"	1
17 February 1965	"Twenty-three Points"	20
28 April 1965	"	4, 7

Several points stand out from this list. First, these documents were too long and complicated for any single editorial to deal with in their entirety. Each editorial, therefore, focused on only one or two major points in the document. Second, People's Daily published a series of editorials on one particular point in a CD before moving on to a different point. This practice would suggest either that these complex programs were implemented in phases and that the editorials reflected this approach, or that the editorials really focused simply on a particular issue that had become a problem in the process of implementation. Third, these editorials concerned a political movement in the rural areas, and the hiatus in their appearance during the fall harvest and spring sowing periods suggests that they in fact were intended as guides to immediate action in the countryside. Political campaigns directly affecting the rural areas in China since 1949 have almost without exception been suspended during the spring sowing and fall harvest. Fourth, the decline in editorials on the last two documents in this series is both obvious and somewhat misleading. There was considerable overlap among these Central Documents, as each modified rather than wholly replaced the previous one. Thus, the diminution in editorial coverage of the documents is at least partly explained by the fact that much of the material in the later CDs had already been covered in earlier ones. Additionally, the research on JMJP editorials with respect to these documents only went up to the end of June 1965 and thus may have missed subsequent editorials published on the "Twenty-three Points." Fifth, these JMJP editorials covered about equally (if one allows for repetition in documents) both CDs that reflected Mao's views and those that posited the other side of the argument. Thus, this dimension of the system was sufficiently institutionalized before the Cultural Revolution that in cases of dispute where each side managed to have its views adopted in CDs over time, People's Daily helped convey the contents of the CDs almost regardless of the internecine fighting behind the scenes. Lastly, the above list shows clearly that only parts of these major Central Documents were conveyed in JMJP editorials while other sections were ignored in this medium.

Thus, before the Cultural Revolution, People's Daily editorials played an important role in communicating the contents of many Central Documents and amplifying the decisions contained in them.[263] These editorials directly addressed problem areas and seemed to have been rather impervious to the politics behind the documents themselves. I have found no examples in these pre-1966 editorials of the JMJP editors actually attempting to undermine the thrust of a major CD recently promulgated by the Party leadership. These editorials in their totality did, however, frequently convey the contents of only portions of a major CD rather than the entire contents of the document.

Often, it should be noted, the JMJP editorial in fact quotes extensively from the Central Document that had sparked it, although the editorial never directly mentions the fact that it is revealing the contents of a recently issued CD. A major segment of the 25 July 1963 editorial, for example, utilizes verbatim the language found in the introduction to the "Former Ten Points." This quoted material runs on for several paragraphs. The same is true for excerpts from Article 9 of the "Former Ten Points" as conveyed in the editorial of 2 June 1963. At other times, the editorial deals directly with the issues raised in one of the articles in the CD but does not use any of the specific language of the document itself. The 28 April 1965 editorial reflecting the contents of Articles 4 and 7 of the "Twenty-three Points" typifies this approach. This is referred to in China as conveying the spirit (ching-shen) of a document.

The role of People's Daily in transmitting and explaining major CDs, moreover, was not limited to the paper's editorials. Rather, short commentaries (tuan-p'ing), unsigned feature articles, and signed feature articles were also often employed. As an example of the latter, an article by Chang P'ing-hua in the 2 November 1964 People's Daily (p. 5) focused on issues raised in Article 1 of the "Revised Later Ten Points," at one point even quoting from this article without naming it. People's Daily also published both NCNA reports on statistics relevant to the problem raised in a CD and various articles on model experiences throughout the country that are in fact relevant to a CD. Sometimes, indeed, these latter have been "model" reports that have been circulated as appendices to the CD itself. Through providing this range of material, People's Daily often played a significant role in communicating and amplifying the contents of Central Documents for a larger audience.

After the Cultural Revolution, by contrast, JMJP generally played a greatly diminshed role in communicating and amplifying CDs for the populace, and in 1974 factional political considerations clearly began to affect what coverage the paper did give to this area. For the years 1970-73 no editorials reflected the contents of any of the available CDs at all,[264] with the minor and insignificant exception of some very general references to "swindlers like Liu Shao-ch'i," "splittists," and so forth, evocative of the Lin Piao affair during the period when the series of CDs on this affair was being issued.

PRC sources have revealed that the radicals gained control over JMJP shortly after the Tenth Party Congress, which convened in August 1973.[265] Almost immediately thereafter, the above pattern changed somewhat. CDs on the campaign to criticize Lin Piao and Confucius were issued on 18 and 22 January[266] and probably subsequently during the course of the spring as well. Then on 2 and 20 February and 15 March JMJP editorials appeared on this campaign, each conveying the radicals' perspective (as did the equivalent CDs). When CD (74) #21 came out on 1 July and refocused the campaign away from the issues dear to the radicals, however, the JMJP editorial of that date turned a deaf ear to its CD counterpart, as analyzed above. Thus, during 1974, the radicals managed to use JMJP editorials to convey their own policy preferences in the first part of the year. During the months prior to July, this meant that the editorials in fact played their pre-Cultural Revolution role vis-à-vis CDs, insofar as the CDs themselves also reflected the radicals' preferences. At mid-year, however, the contents of the CDs changed, and editorial support for the Central Documents immediately ceased. Only once from mid-1974 to the end of 1975 did a JMJP editorial seem to reflect the contents of a CD--when the 11 March 1975 editorial evidently evoked some of the spirit of the CD on railway transportation.

Other dimensions of People's Daily guidance in carrying out the policies contained in Central Documents also seem to have deteriorated after the Cultural Revolution, presumably reflecting an attempt by Yao Wen-yuan and his colleagues to mitigate the force of policy directives with which they disagreed. An intensive review of JMJP coverage during the months following the issuance of CD (74) #21, for example, finds few articles that come squarely to grips with the issues raised in the CD and provide concrete guidance on how to handle the problems encountered. A former PRC cadre who examined these articles termed them "vacuous" (k'ung-tung-ti), and comparison of these with the equivalent People's Daily coverage before the Cultural Revolution simply highlights the vast change that seems to have occurred during this period.

Treatment of CDs in the provincial media seems to have varied somewhat according to the political ties of the provincial leadership, as illustrated by the analysis of the transmission of CD (74) #21 above. Clearly, though, the media in many provinces continued to present the kind of amplification and guidance that JMJP and they had together provided before the GPCR. Thus, for instance, the provincial newspapers of the following provinces carried editorials that actually reflected CD (74) #21: Inner Mongolian Autonomous Region, Fukien, Shantung, Kiangsu, Hunan, Szechwan, Heilungkiang, Sinkiang, and Yunnan.[267] Virtually all of these editorials quoted directly, and often extensively, from the text of CD (74) #21, albeit without indicating that these sections were direct quotations. In the other ways analyzed above, however, some of these editorials twisted the letter and/or the spirit of the original document. The supporting feature articles, reports, and model experiences conveyed in the provincial papers of these months did likewise.

In sum, the process of transmitting the contents of Central Documents is complex and flexible. It begins by a diffusion of the document itself to a selected group of units for study and implementation. It then may lead to an increasingly widely ramifying set of efforts to communicate the contents of the document to wider circles of people. This transmission process is one that proceeds roughly step-by-step from the highest to the lowest levels of the system and also tends to move from the "inside" to the "outside"--i.e., from Party cadres to other civil servants to the public. The dissemination of a particular document is cut off at the point stipulated by the authorities who issue it.

Generally, the original CD only circulates to the limited group of units on the <u>chu-sung chi-kuan</u> list. Further transmaission, which can utilize a rather bewildering variety of vehicles, frequently carries increasingly truncated versions of the document downward. This process of continual summarization and condensation during transmission increases the likelihood that periods of political conflict will produce efforts to distort the thrust of a document, by omission if nothing else. It also means that since many of these documents are broad in scope and cover a substantial range of issues in their various articles, the people in one locale might be briefed on the subtance of some articles while those in another place are being given information from a quite different set of articles. People at the basic levels in different provinces thus might well receive very different pictures of what is in fact the same document. Another possible method of distortion, as noted above, relies on transmitting the contents of several CDs to lower levels and the public at once.

The only systematic change in the transmission process clearly evident from this research is in the role that <u>People's Daily</u> plays in this process. Before the Cultural Revolution, <u>JMJP</u> gave guidance from the Center on the issues raised in major CDs, but after the GPCR this virtually ceased to be the case (the evidence is not yet available on whether <u>JMJP</u> has reverted to its previous role since the arrest of the Gang of Four--most importantly, of Yao Wen-yuan--in October 1976). Political factionalism clearly affected the relationship between <u>People's Daily</u> and Central Documents during the year or so after the Gang of

Four gained control over JMJP in late 1973. This does not seem to have been the case for any year before the Cultural Revolution. Thus, the findings of this research effort support and lend concrete substance to the widely held belief that the moderates basically controlled the executive organs of the Party during the early and mid-1970s while the radicals had to rely on their leverage over JMJP and several other media outlets to blunt the thrust of the decisions taken by their adversaries within the councils of the Party. In a real sense, then, the political strife of the 1970s caused a deterioration in the process by which the Central leadership transmitted the contents of its decisions and provided guidance on their implementation.

IV. CONCLUSION
CENTRAL DOCUMENTS AND POLITBURO POLITICS

Mao Tse-tung sculpted the initial Central Document system so as to achieve a range of goals. He wanted to find an efficient way to centralize ultimate decision making power in Peking while still conceding necessary flexibility to local political units. He sought to enable leading generalists of the system to absorb and utilize the information generated by specialized bureaucracies without becoming overwhelmed by the bureaucracies themselves. In addition, Mao tried to insure that he personally would remain astride the document flow between the Central Committee and lower levels of the political hierarchy, able to use the system of bureaucratic rules to serve his personal political needs while not being tightly hemmed in by the system itself. The product of these considerations was the Central Document system analyzed in the body of this volume.

This system often works in a way that brings into play the major interested parties, including the institutional actors concerned, during the process of drafting Central Documents on important issues. Typically, well before the full Politburo reaches a decision on a topic, one or more of the major bureaucracies in that issue area is called upon to contribute to the drafting of an appropriate policy paper. Geographically defined bureaucratic interests may also be drawn into this process, and initial drafts are revised repeatedly as additional views become known. Indeed, the drafting procedure not infrequently even includes tapping a limited sample of public opinion via "investigations" of the situation in local areas. Once policy papers have been drawn up and reviewed, moreover, many major issues are referred to a central work conference or other Central meetings, where relatively freewheeling discussion of the topic and options can take place among a broad range of Central and provincial Party leaders. Clearly, in the Chinese political system as in others, these trappings of consultation and discussion can be made hollow in the final analysis if the recommendations they produce are flouted by the final decision makers, as seems to have occurred at certain periods in the PRC.[268] Still, the system itself is one that is designed to bring interested parties into the decision making process so that deliberations can be undertaken with a full understanding of the factual and political dimensions of the problem concerned.

The input of the various actors is structured by the assignment of specific functional areas of responsibility within the Politburo and the organization of the Party and state bureaucracies into functional "systems" on a national basis. This arrangement can be seen as a rational and efficient way to link up the Politburo with the various bureaucracies that govern China. The rules governing the flow of documents, and thus of information, are contoured to this functional division of responsibility. Nothing in this modus operandi need preclude widespread sharing of information and full cooperation among various members of the Politburo. As documented in the text above, however, to the degree that the Politburo itself becomes divided and ridden with factionalism, this system of channeling information can provide a vehicle by which each side can try to deny necessary technical and political data to its opponents. Indeed, the rules of this system allow for a situation whereby, until policy papers concerning a given issue area are virtually complete, only perhaps one or two Politburo leaders and the Politburo member responsible for that "system" of work need have access to the drafting process and the information that it generates.[269] This is a system that can be used, then, to work against those who would like to block a policy in a functional area over which they have not been given control, for they cannot legitimately undertake independent investigations of the issue or begin to work seriously on the problem until it has been formally tabled for discussion by the entire Politburo.

Where dissension within the Politburo is great, then, this arrangement, not surprisingly, affects the political strategies of the leaders who participate in it. An important part of "politics" becomes the ability to "capture" an issue area. To do so has important advantages. It allows the Politburo member concerned to bring to bear the bureaucratic resources under his control and to generate data pertinent to the issue area. He can do so, moreover, early in the decision making process rather than only near its completion. He also enjoys legitimate access to the document flow in that functional system, thereby gaining a great deal of information about the problems and prospects in that arena. And finally, securing control over an issue area permits the Politburo member concerned to place questions concerning that issue area on the agenda of the top leadership, thus enhancing his ability to shape that agenda for his own political purposes. Thus it is not surprising that Lin Piao joined with Chiang Ch'ing to try to "capture" issues in the cultural realm by staging a Forum on Literature and Art for Troops in February 1966, or that Chiang Ch'ing herself in 1975 tried to extend her sway to include at least a portion of the foreign trade system by using her control over the cultural realm to criticize art objects and handicrafts being exported by the PRC.[270]

This responsibility system places a premium on a political faction's being able to place at least one of its supporters into each of the major functional hierarchies, for by this means the leaders of the faction can gain (illegitimate) access to items of interest in the document flow from each functional area. Lacking these cohorts astride the various document streams, even Politburo membership does not provide a means for the factional leaders to learn what is taking place--and what is being planned--in functional areas about which they are concerned but for which they have no assigned responsibility. The importance of this strategem emerged clearly in the above case study of the radicals' strategy for blocking the adoption of the "Outline Summary Report on the Work of the Academy of Sciences."

In sum, the responsibility system can dictate to an important degree the institutional resources available to individuals and factions in the Politburo and their prerogatives in the policy making process. This system itself, consequently, may become an important target of the political strategies adopted by the Politburo members as they try to affect the outcome of Chinese politics.

Our analysis of the Central Document series makes clear that the Politburo does in fact handle an extremely broad range of issues, justifying its image as the nerve center of the Chinese political system. It also illuminates the fact, however, that most Politburo decisions are intended to be followed in spirit rather than in letter. Thus, not only is there ample room for politics in the normally consultative and incremental policy making system in China, but this latitude for political maneuver clearly extends to the transmission and implementation phases of many policy issues. In China as in the United States, in brief, a "decision" by the highest level leaders often merely sets the framework for the next stage in the battle over policy.

While the skeletal outline of the system for transmitting Central Documents conforms to our image that once a decision is made, it flows from the higher levels to lower levels and from the Party core "outward," there are nevertheless some key characteristics of this system that allow considerable room for political maneuvering at virtually all stages of the process. Naturally, the very flexibility in implementation intended in most CDs, and the fact that many of these documents prescribe a broad range of actions to cope with a problem, combine to delineate an area of sometimes considerable discretion in determining how best to contour the policy dictated by the Center to the conditions in the local areas. Other less purposeful characteristics of the transmission system, however, create additional unintended room for making policy in the process of transmitting Central decisions.

The sheer volume of Central Documents, averaging about three per month, permits lower level cadres to group several CDs together in the transmission process if conditions warrant (e.g., during the busy season in agriculture or when several CDs are sent out almost simultaneously). Such "telescoping" of documents can be used effectively to expand the range of issues on the locale's agenda at any one time, thereby increasing the local leadership's discretion as to the emphasis that should be given to any particular task. Some local leaders might thereby blunt the thrust of a CD they find not to their liking while seeming to remain well within the boundaries of legitimate discretion in view of local conditions. This tactic of combining several CDs in the transmission process is clearly an inviting ploy when the Central leadership has just changed the thrust of policy on the issue concerned, such as was the case with CD (74) #21 on the campaign to criticize Lin Piao and Confucius.

A range of considerations requires that the contents of many Central Documents be summarized and condensed as the documents flow down the transmission belt. Lower levels of political interest and sophistication, security and political concerns, and simply the volume of information transmitted via the Central Document channel all dictate that at lower levels most people must receive only a summary of the original document rather than its full text. This process of condensation and summarization itself, however, again permits the exercise of discretion in ways that can have significant policy consequences. It is evidently not unusual, for instance, for a single Central Document to look quite different by the time it is presented to the masses in two different provinces. There is, then, considerable room for "adjusting" the contents and implications of a Central Document during the transmission process by taking full advantage of the flexibility built into this system without clearly violating any of its rules.

The picture revealed by a study of Central Documents thus indicates that the Chinese have developed a flexible system, one that can be reasonably well attuned to realizing the twin goals of having a few top leaders make the key decisions across a wide range of issue areas while at the same time having these decisions implemented in ways that take adequate account of local conditions. This system allows for both an impressive degree of discipline and centralization as well as considerable "give." Well-placed individuals and groups can generate opportunities to influence policy outcomes at virtually every stage of the decision making process, which is certainly as it should be if the system is to make decisions that do not lose touch with the complexities of the Chinese scene.

The data presented in this paper on the situation since the Cultural Revolution, however, provide striking and concrete evidence to support the general image that the institutions and operation of the system seriously eroded in recent years. To use Samuel Huntington's apt phrase, for more than a decade now the Chinese system has been experiencing "political decay." One senses, indeed, the anguish this caused among many leaders in the current denunciations of the Gang of Four, a number of which focus on the ways in which this group violated the bureaucratic rules analyzed in this text.

Mao Tse-tung launched a frontal attack on the Chinese Communist Party during the Cultural Revolution, and the resulting extreme factionalism that characterized the Chinese leadership during the early and mid-1970s made every dimension of the Central Document network a battleground, the effects of which were to erode the system itself.[271] One senses that the practice of channeling information within one functional hierarchy became more than ever a means for hoarding that information and denying it to one's political adversaries. The battle extended to the division of responsibility among Politburo members themselves, with each group trying to expand the range of functional systems under its control. This dimension of Politburo intrigue may partly explain why the fragmentary evidence on the functional responsibilities of various Politburo members during the past half decade has conveyed an image of almost kaleidoscopic changes--with Hua Kuo-feng, for instance, variously being assigned to agriculture, public security, science and technology, and the administration of the State Council before the events of 1976. Indeed, given the overrepresentation of radicals on the Politburo, this concern may partially explain why the moderate leaders in the Politburo allowed this body to be staffed in a way that permitted less direct control of some major functional areas by the Politburo than had been the case prior to the Cultural Revolution. Looked at from a somewhat different angle, the Cultural Revolution clearly produced a Politburo whose membership was determined by factional political considerations rather than out of concern to exercise direct leadership over the full range of major functional systems in China. This "distortion" of the Politburo roster has been partially, but seemingly not completely, rectified by the changes in Politburo membership made by the first plenum of the Eleventh Central Committee in August 1977.[272]

Other tactics pursued by high level leaders also chipped away at the integrity of the Politburo system of dividing responsibility. Three in particular stand out. First, Chiang Ch'ing is accused of having tried to communicate directly with certain units in the PLA rather than going through the military system headed by Yeh Chien-ying.[273] This attempt to bypass the normal communications system by direct liaison with the subordinate units in another Politburo member's area of functional responsibility may well have been also characteristic of both other radicals and their moderate opponents. A second important tactic to evade the constraints of the responsibility system was to try to "capture" an issue so that it could be handled by the bureaucratic units one controlled, as described above. The third basic tactic, also reviewed above, was to place loyal subordinates into the functional bureaucracies controlled by one's opponents. The widespread use of these three strategems by the radicals--and to an extent also by the moderates[274]--went far toward disrupting the normal functioning of the policy making system during the early 1970s. These tactics were not new. Indeed, Mao Tse-tung had used all of them himself in his quest to maximize his influence in the Chinese policy process.[275] What distinguished the post-Cultural Revolution period is the frequency of their employment by factions in the Politburo and the damage this did to the system itself.

Indeed, given the radicals' access to the media and other publications facilities, the tactic of placing one's subordinates in a range of functional bureaucracies became an especially crucial part of their larger strategy, for one of their key ploys was to leak information surreptitiously obtained from these "plants" to the public (and to Mao?) in selective excerpts which could then serve as the basis for launching a political campaign based on the "issues" concerned. By having their followers dispersed throughout the various functional systems, therefore, the radicals could pursue a strategy of preemption, not having to wait until the policy they opposed had been fully developed and a great deal of support among interested parties already mobilized during the drafting process before they could go into action.

The radicals found that they lost out in policy debates more often than they won. This, in turn, reflected the fact that they exercised control over relatively few of the functional systems. They tried, therefore, to reduce the authority with which the Party Center spoke to the rest of the system by not allowing the resources of the Central media to be brought into play in support of the policies they opposed. Yao Wen-yuan undoubtedly played the critical role in this effort, and his use of the media ran directly counter to pre-Cultural Revolution norms. Before 1966, as demonstrated in the review of the Socialist Education Campaign CDs presented above, the People's Daily often played an important role in supporting and amplifying the decisions of the Center no matter what kind of high level conflict had been involved over these decisions. Yao, by contrast, typically simply failed to print information in People's Daily that supported the policies he opposed, and occasionally he actually printed materials (such as the 1 July 1974 editorial examined in the text) that partially undermined the thrust of a CD. Central Documents that the radicals supported, by contrast, seem to have enjoyed pre-Cultural Revolution type support and amplification in People's Daily. Thus, after the Cultural Revolution the Center no longer could speak with one coordinated voice both "in house" and through its channels of public communication, a fact which, not surprisingly, made it somewhat easier for lower level cadres to frustrate the intentions of the Politburo as expressed in CDs. Thus, in a very real sense the power of the Politburo diminished in the system.

In sum, the information generated by this study of the Central Document system graphically reveals that after the Cultural Revolution in a range of ways the Politburo lost some of its integrity as an institution and a portion of its capacity to handle the issues of the day. The constant threat of unwarranted leaks impaired the ability of its members to draft and present policy papers. The membership of the Politburo itself reflected less the functional requirements of the institution than the factional loyalties of its members. Political conflict within the Politburo meant that there were constant attempts to prevent policy papers that were being drafted from actually coming up for final consideration and that many of those that did make it to this stage fell victim to politically motivated attacks. The constant mushrooming of new political campaigns meant further delays in the drafting of key documents, as these had to be reworked to take account of the latest political twists and turns. In this atmosphere, moreover, lower level cadres were emboldened to take maximum advantage of the flexibility built into the system, especially since many of them knew that they could enjoy a measure of protection from kindred spirits in Peking. The Central media became less closely coordinated with--and supportive of--the decisions communicated internally via Central Documents, highlighting once again for the local leaders the degree to which the Party Center was torn by strife. Indeed, as judged by the stream of CDs on Lin Piao, Teng Hsiao-p'ing, and the Gang of Four, the CD system itself seems to have become increasingly involved in communicating information about political struggles and purges and somewhat less concerned with other substantive issues. The deterioration in the system of Central Documents, then, reflects the institutional decay of the larger political system of which it is a part.

Teng Hsiao-p'ing and Hua Kuo-feng were key actors in this system during the mid-1970s, and the case studies of the 1975 documents on science and technology and on industry presented in the text strongly suggest that these two men are fully committed to the system of Central Documents as that system seems to have worked in the period before the Cultural Revolution. We can, therefore, expect major efforts on their part to reestablish the system analyzed in this monograph, including a clear division of responsibility for most members of the Politburo,[276] an incremental and highly consultative process of document drafting, the convening of central work conferences to consider important issues, and the full use of People's Daily and the other Central media to support and amplify the messages being sent out via the Central Document system.

Conflict, however, has not disappeared from the Chinese political system. It is likely, indeed, that what we have witnessed to date is merely the first stage in the succession to Mao Tse-tung, with additional significant leadership changes yet to come. Of the five key people who now hold "generalist" positions on the Politburo, for example, all but Hua Kuo-feng and Wang Tung-hsing are in their seventies or older. Some younger members of the Politburo, such as Ch'en Hsi-lien, Li Te-sheng, and Wu Teh, have clearly been intricately involved in the factional politics of the past and may well run into serious trouble in the future. Changing coalitions and perhaps factionalism will thus continue to characterize Peking politics for probably at least the rest of this decade. If there is one major lesson to be learned from the present analysis of Central Documents, it is that the system of rules and procedures analyzed in this text will affect both the strategies and fortunes of the actors in this drama. To understand fully what is occurring in elite politics in Peking, then, analysts must remain sensitive not only to the policy issues under debate but also to the institutional setting within which they are contested.

NOTES

1. See, for instance, Edward Rice, Mao's Way (Berkeley: University of California Press, 1972).

2. For example, David M. Lampton, The Politics of Medicine in China: The Policy Process, 1949-1977 (Boulder: Westview Press, 1977).

3. Michel Oksenberg, "The Chinese Policy Process and the Public Health Issue: An Arena Approach," Studies in Comparative Communism 7, no. 4 (Winter 1974): 375-408 (hereafter cited as Oksenberg, "Arena").

4. Kenneth Lieberthal, Research Guide to Central Party and Government Meetings in China, 1949-1975 (White Plains, N.Y.: International Arts and Sciences Press, 1976).

5. Since at least 1967 all Central Documents have borne the label chung-fa (literally, "centrally issued"). Only one pre-Cultural Revolution CD available in the West has a chung-fa label, however--"Some Problems Currently Arising in the Course of the Rural Socialist Education Movement," in R. Baum and F. Teiwes, Ssu-Ch'ing: The Socialist Education Movement, China Research Monograph No. 2 (Berkeley: University of California Press, 1968), pp. 118-26 (hereafter cited as the "Twenty-three Points"). The chung-fa label on this document appears only on the original Chinese text. I am grateful to Richard Baum for providing me with a copy of this text. It is simply unclear whether the chung-fa label came into wide use only in 1967 or whether it has been put on all Central Documents since the 1950s. The latter possibility cannot be ruled out, as most texts of Central Documents available in the West are based on copies of these documents rather than on the originals. In some instances, the title of a CD is not available even when the text is known in the West.

6. On the Eleventh Politburo, for instance, Hua Kuo-feng is simultaneously premier of the State Council; Yeh Chien-ying is minister of defense; Teng Hsiao-p'ing is chief of staff; Li Hsien-nien is vice-premier of the State Council; Wang Tung-hsing heads the Party General Office; Yü Ch'iu-li heads the State Planning Commission; Fang I is vice-president of the Chinese Academy of Sciences; and so forth. The above represents only a partial and illustrative listing of the concomitant offices held as of the time of this writing.

7. Two analyses by Michel Oksenberg provide perceptive insights into the modes and implications of these shifts: "The Political Leader," in Mao Tse-tung in the Scales of History, ed. Dick Wilson (London: Cambridge University Press, 1977); and "Arena," pp. 384-94.

8. For instance, of the eight decisions regarding agricultural procurement for the years 1954-1960 published in the Chung-Hua Jen-min Kung-ho-kuo fa-kuei hui-pien, four were issued by a government organ alone (the State Council or Ministry of Food) and four were put out jointly by the State Council and the Central Committee of the Party. Three of the four jointly issued decrees were published in 1959-60. These decisions are listed in: Tao-tai Hsia, Guide to Selected Legal Sources of Mainland China (Washington, D.C.: Library of Congress, 1967), nos. 523, 652, 880, 972, 1202, 1365, 1467, and 1584 respectively. More impressionistically, the number of jointly issued decrees in the Fa-kuei hui-pien seems to increase for the period 1958-63, although the degree to which this may be an artifact of changes in editorial policy for this series is unclear.

9. See especially: Michel Oksenberg, "Policy Making under Mao, 1949-1968: An Overview," in China: Management of a Revolutionary Society, ed. John M. H. Lindbeck (Seattle: University of Washington Press, 1971), pp. 79-115.

10. This is documented in the case study below on the "Outline Summary Report on the Work in the Academy of Sciences," p. 42.

11. Appendix II provides a full list of known CDs since 1966.

12. Most that have been officially released are printed in the Chung-Hua Jen-min Kung-ho-kuo fa-kuei hui-pien, published roughly semi-annually for September 1954—December 1963. Only a small percentage of the Central Documents passed during these years are contained in these volumes, however.

13. Since the PRC ceased publishing the Chung-Hua Jen-min Kung-ho-kuo fa-kuei hui-pien at the end of 1963, probably fewer State Council documents and documents from the ministries, commissions, and departments than Central Documents have become available outside China because, due to their technical nature and narrow focus, they are more likely to remain completely inside the bureaucracies in the PRC. Thus, foreign intelligence has less opportunity to gain access to these documents.

14. This sketch of the regulations governing official documents is based on interviews. The rules themselves are classified in the PRC.

15. Except for communications from the CCP General Office. See, for instance, CCP Documents of the Great Proletarian Cultural Revolution, 1966-1967 (Kowloon: Union Research Institute, 1968), pp. 143-44 (hereafter cited as CR Docs).

16. CR Docs, pp. 77-80, 137-42.

17. Ibid., pp. 107-12, 125-30, 147-54.

18. Ibid., pp. 113-20.

19. Text in Documents of the Chinese Communist Party Central Committee, September 1956–April 1959 (Kowloon: Union Research Institute, 1971) pp. 695-726 (document hereafter cited as the "Sixty Points on Communes," book hereafter cited as CC Docs). An earlier version of this CD had been circulated in May 1961.

20. A brief description of these issues is provided in Lieberthal, Research Guide, pp. 188-92. Byung-joon Ahn provides a more detailed analysis of these questions in his Chinese Politics and the Cultural Revolution (Seattle: University of Washington Press, 1976), chapter 4.

21. A summary of the contents of this document is given in CC Docs, pp. 689-94.

22. Text in CC Docs, pp. 677-80.

23. Yunnan Radio, 27 February 1977--FBIS/PRC, 1 March 1977, J-3.

24. See, for instance, CD(67)#117 (issued on 1 April 1967), which transmits and amplifies on the 27 March 1967 Central Committee decision on the question of Anhwei: CR Docs, pp. 389-401.

25. See, for instance, the Central Committee comment on the 16 September 1967 telegram of the Kirin Provincial Committee in CR Docs, pp. 81-82.

26. CR Docs, p. 92.

27. The Rural Work Department of the Central Committee has not been identified in the Chinese media since the Cultural Revolution. The media have, indeed, revealed the existence of only four Central Committee departments since the late 1960s: International Liaison, Organization, Propaganda and United Front Work.

28. Ying-mao Kau, The Lin Piao Affair (White Plains, N.Y.: International Arts and Sciences Press, 1975), pp. 69-70.

29. Mentioned in Kau, pp. 56, 79. Several Central Documents in the last few months of 1971 had provided some additional information on this issue.

30. Text in Kau, pp. 78-95. Issued on 13 January 1972.

31. Text in Kau, pp. 55-66. Issued on 17 March 1972.

32. Text in Kau, pp. 96-105. Issued on 2 July 1972.

33. Partial text in Kau, pp. 118-21. Issued in September 1972.

34. Text of CD in Kau, pp. 110-17. The dating of the approval strongly suggests that this report was discussed and adopted at a Central Work Conference preceding the Tenth Party Congress (24-28 August). It then formed the basis for Chou En-lai's report at the Congress, and the Congress probably secretly gave its imprimatur to the acceptance of the full report as a CD and its circulation within the Party.

35. In late 1976, early 1977, and on 5 January and 3 May 1977. See, respectively, Ming Pao, 15 March 1977; AFP Hong Kong, 17 March 1977--FBIS/PRC, 17 March 1977, E-1-2; Ibid.; and Ming Pao, 27 May 1977.

36. Ming Pao, 27 May 1977.

37. Ming Pao, 29 March 1977--FBIS/PRC, 30 March 1977, N-1.

38. See respectively: Chung-kung yen-chiu 11, no. 7 (1977), pp. 103-60; and Ming Pao, 2 April 1977.

39. CR Docs presents a list, with accompanying explanations, on pp. ii-iii. Pertinent additional information is available in: Central People's Government Council, Kung-wen ch'u-li chih-hsing pan-fa; Hsia kung-wen shou-ts'e, ed. Su Fan; and Kung-wen ti chi-pen chih-shih, ed. Meng Ping and Hsia Li.

40. See, for example, CR Docs, pp. 351-60. This information comes from one of my informants.

41. See, for example, CR Docs, pp. 501-10.

42. CR Docs places a t'ung-ling (circular order) between ming-ling and chüeh-ting (p. ii). We omit discussion of t'ung-ling because it is much less used than ming-ling and chüeh-ting.

43. For example, the major document initiating the Cultural Revolution in August 1966 was labeled a chüeh-ting; see CR Docs, pp. 33-55.

44. Texts of these are provided in CR Docs, pp. 219-24 (Chekiang); 385-91 (Tsinghai); 415-20 (Inner Mongolian Autonomous Region, or IMAR); 431-38 (Szechwan); 583-88 (Kwangtung); and 603-8 (Kwangsi).

45. Text in CR Docs, pp. 255-61.

46. Text in CR Docs, pp. 131-35.

47. Text in CR Docs, pp. 319-24.

48. See note 19 above.

49. See, for example, CR Docs, pp. 113-20 (draft chih-shih); and pp. 341-46 (draft kuei-ting).

50. This "reporting back" (hui-pao) process is characteristic of the implementation of all documents. See Michel Oksenberg, "Methods of Communication within the Bureaucracy," China Quarterly, no. 57 (January-March 1974): 1-39 (hereafter cited as Oksenberg, "Communication").

51. Texts in Baum and Teiwes, pp. 72-94 and 102-17 respectively. The revised draft was in turn modified by a document specifying twenty-three "problems" in the campaign that Mao pushed through in January 1965 (text in ibid., pp. 118-26). The fact that the two drafts were themselves reflective of deep policy differences at the Center does not detract from the points made in the text about "drafts" in general. On the larger policy differences concerning these particular drafts, see R. Baum, Prelude to Revolution (New York: Columbia University Press, 1975), chapters 2 and 4.

52. Victor Falkenheim, "Provincial Administration in Fukien, 1944-1966" (Ph.D. dissertation, Columbia University, 1971), pp. 248-53; and CR Docs, pp. ii-iii provide the best available information on these additional types of documents.

53. Texts in CR Docs, pp. 13-28 and 33-54 respectively.

54. Text in CR Docs, p. 129. It is likely that the version of the CD displayed in public places lacked the identifying serial number, the specification of organs for internal circulation, and the Central Committee chop--all of which formed parts of the original document.

55. Oksenberg provides some information on the courier system in "Communication."

56. Some sense of the disruption in the State Council is conveyed in Donald Klein, "The State Council and the Cultural Revolution," China Quarterly, no. 35 (July–September 1968): 78-95.

57. If consistent use of the "chung-fa" label began only in 1967, the personalization of Mao's authority by then may provide a partial explanation. "Chung-fa" (literally, "issued by the Center") is nicely ambiguous--the "chung" may refer to the Central Committee or simply to a noninstitutionalized Center.

58. For example, CD#18 on 18 October 1976 providing guidance for removing pictures and references to the Gang of Four: Chung-yang jih-pao, 10 November 1976.

59. CD(76)#1 announced the appointment of Hua Kuo-feng as acting premier of the State Council: JMJP, 3 June 1977--FBIS/PRC, 6 June 1977, E-16.

60. Indeed, the Chinese have alleged that during Mao's final months Mao Yuan-hsin, a partisan of the Gang of Four, controlled access to the Party Chairman: NYT, 30 October 1977, p. 11. This would imply that Mao Yuan-hsin may have prevented Mao Tse-tung from seeing draft CDs that were sent to him for his approval. As noted below, however, Mao ordered in 1953 that no CDs could go out without his approval--an order which may well have remained in effect until his death. This, then, may help explain the fall-off of CDs in 1976.

61. On these events and the related debate, see Kenneth Lieberthal, "Strategies of Conflict in China during 1975-76," Contemporary China (December 1976): 7-14.

62. Mao Tse-tung hsüan-chi, vol. 5 (Peking: 1977), p. 80. Mao issued this order on 19 May 1953.

63. Text in CR Docs, pp. 3-12.

64. See the summary of the May conference in Lieberthal, Research Guide, pp. 248-50.

65. Peking Chingkangshan (Editorial Office, Chingkangshan, Tsinghua University Center of Red Guards Congress), 27 May 1967--Survey of China Mainland Press--Supplement, no. 195 (31 July 1967): 24.

66. For example, see the CDs in CR Docs, pp. 407-11, 457-59.

67. During the Cultural Revolution there were charges made that Liu Shao-ch'i had issued documents in the name of the Central Committee without Mao's approval. No evidence is available to support or refute these charges.

68. The account of this incident is given in NCNA English, 18 March 1977--FBIS/PRC, 18 March 1977, E-4.

69. As mentioned in note 27 above, no such Central Committee department has been identified since the Cultural Revolution. This need not mean that no such department currently exists, however.

70. For example, CD (74) #21 on grasping revolution and promoting production during the campaign to criticize Lin Piao and Confucius

produced demands in some provinces that the highest-ranking official and his immediate subordinate in all Party committees must assume personal responsibility for carrying out the tasks of the CD. See, for example, Yunnan Radio, 6 July 1974--FBIS/PRC, 8 July 1974, J-5.

71. Text in CC Docs, pp. 681-83.

72. Ibid., p. 682.

73. Before the GPCR, it is not completely clear whether the Central Committee Secretariat or the General Office of the CCP would have handled this type of problem. I suspect it was the latter. Examples of documents issued by the CCP General Office are available in CR Docs, pp. 95-99, 143-44 and 511-34.

74. Most of these that are available for 1966-67 are published in CR Docs.

75. See pp. 9-10 above.

76. It is worth recalling, however, that not all issues are handled only via bureaucratic communications. The leadership in the past has also used the media, remarks made on personal inspection trips, and other vehicles for communicating views on pertinent issues.

77. See Appendix II.

78. It is also possible, of course, that the decision to communicate a document via the Central Document network in some instances may not be made until the document actually comes before the leadership for final approval.

79. See, for example, CR Docs, pp. 81-82.

80. See CR Docs, pp. 73-76.

81. Mao's techniques of communicating his desires to the Party are analyzed in Michel Oksenberg, "Policy Making under Mao," pp. 79-115.

82. That this division of responsibility system has always existed is supported by considerable documentary evidence and the testimony

of one observer with whom I discussed the issue during a 1977 visit to the PRC. The system was officially decreed for all Party committees in Article 11 of the Party Constitution passed by the Eleventh Party Congress on 18 August 1977 (text in FBIS/PRC Supplement, 1 September 1977, pp. 63-71).

83. Byung-joon Ahn, "Adjustments in the Great Leap Forward and Their Ideological Legacy, 1959-62," in Ideology and Politics in Contemporary China, ed. Chalmers Johnson (Seattle: University of Washington Press, 1973), pp. 275-80.

84. Kirin Radio, 28 September 1977--FBIS/PRC, 5 October 1977, L-3.

85. Wan shan hung p'ien (Peking: Workers, Peasants and Soldiers Literature and Art Commune of Peking, April 1967)--SCMM-S, no. 33 (20 February 1969): 9.

86. Text in CR Docs, pp. 3-12. The process of drafting the "Outline Report" and having it adopted is portrayed, as noted above, in Chingkangshan (Editorial Office, Chingkangshan, Tsinghua University Center of Red Guards Congress, 27 May 1967)--SCMP-S, no. 195 (31 July 1967): 20-28.

87. These issues and the supporting documentation are presented in detail in Lieberthal, Research Guide, pp. 236-49. The channeling of authority in the battle for control of this issue is actually somewhat more complex even than that presented in the text. P'eng Chen had two legitimate points of access to the issue: he headed the Five-man Cultural Revolution Group, through which he had responsibility for cultural policy; and he was mayor of Peking, where Wu Han served as first vice-mayor. P'eng used both these points in his quest for control over the issue, as witnessed by his repeatedly convening meetings for both the Cultural Revolution Group and the Peking People's Council to deal with the issue. Lin Piao, by contrast, had to have the Military Affairs Committee adopt the "Forum Summary" and then submit it for consideration as a CD. See ibid., pp. 11-13.

88. I am grateful to Allen Whiting for bringing this information to my attention.

89. This is pieced together from JMJP, 20 June 1977--FBIS/PRC, 1 July 1977, E-7; K'ang Li and Yen Feng, "The Circumstances Surrounding the Appearance of the 'Outline Summary Report,'"

Hsüeh-hsi yü p'i-p'an, no. 4 (14 April 1976): 20-27--SPRCM, no. 870 (10 May 1976): 16-28. More details on this process are provided in the case study of the "Outline Summary Report" below.

90. Ahn, "Adjustments," pp. 277-78. It is possible that prior to the demise of the Central Committee Secretariat, its members likewise had the authority to draft CDs in their own issue areas.

91. JMJP, 17 March 1977--FBIS/PRC, 31 March 1977, E-4. JMJP put it this way: The Chiang Ch'ing-commissioned "The Battle of Hsisha" was named "a 'poem report' because if it were named a poem, the reader might have considered it fiction, and if it were termed a report, it would have been impossible to have Chiang Ch'ing's own stuff incorporated into it."

92. Or, before the Cultural Revolution, on the Secretariat.

93. See, for instance, the drafting process regarding educational policy in Ahn, "Adjustments," pp. 279-80.

94. In a variant of this, Politburo members themselves carry out consultations and/or local investigations: Oksenberg, "Communications," pp. 21-26.

95. Liu Shao-ch'i, for instance, repeatedly used Tientsin as a testing point for his policies. The fact that Liu's wife is a Tientsin native with extensive family connections in the city probably helped assure Liu of the loyalty that he required from the local leaders in order to use the city in this way. See Kenneth Lieberthal, "Tientsin," in Provincial Handbook to the PRC, ed. Edwin Winckler (Stanford: Stanford University Press, forthcoming). For P'eng Chen, not surprisingly, the Peking municipal environs served a similar function. See Byung-joon Ahn, Chinese Politics and the Cultural Revolution (Seattle: University of Washington Press, 1976).

96. For partial stenographic reports on two of these meetings, see: Mao Tse-tung ssu-hsiang wan-sui (1967), pp. 578-97--translated in Miscellany of Mao Tse-tung Thought (JPRS, nos. 612691-2, 1974), pp. 408-26, for a 20 December 1964 meeting on the draft "Twenty-three Points" on the Socialist Education Movement; and Ch'i Hsin, Ssu-jen-pang shih-chien t'an-so (Hong Kong: Ch'i-shih nien-tai tsa-chih she, April 1977), pp. 194-200--SPRCM, no. 926

(23 May 1977): 37-42, for a 26 September 1975 meeting on the draft "Outline Summary Report on the Work of the Chinese Academy of Sciences."

97. If he so desires, the Politburo member can make these comments in writing, without convening a meeting at all.

98. For example, the first draft of Mao Tse-tung's "Twelve-Year National Program for the Development of Agriculture" contained eleven articles, the second draft contained seventeen, and the final draft contained forty: Mao Tse-tung ssu-hsiang wan-sui (1967), p. 150--Miscellany, p. 81. The first draft of the "Eight Points on Literature and Art" contained ten points: Ahn, "Adjustments." Also, the 1975 document "Some Questions on Accelerating the Development of Industry" went through six major revisions and thirty-two minor alterations before it was deemed ready to be put forward for adoption: Kung Hsiao-wen, "Teng Hsiao-p'ing and the 'Twenty Articles,'" Hsüeh-hsi yü p'i-p'an, no. 6 (1976): 14--SPRCM, no. 879 (12 July 1976): 1.

99. Or to present a skewed but realistic and detailed reconstruction--replete with direct quotes--to serve current political needs. See, for instance, the very different (but factually compatible) partial reconstructions of the drafting process for the "Outline Summary Report on the Work of the Academy of Sciences" presented in K'ang Li and Yen Feng's article (cited above) and in JMJP, 30 June 1977--FBIS/PRC, 1 July 1977, E-6-15.

100. One speck of evidence does indicate that CDs are typically formally approved by the Politburo at its regular meetings before they are chopped and circulated. This evidence consists of the coincidence that data on public appearances of Politburo members during the period 1958-59 (when the press gave very extensive coverage to their activities) strongly suggest that a Politburo meeting convened roughly every nine days during that period, while the available data on CDs for the 1970s indicate, as noted above, that one is normally adopted about every ten days. Although this evidence is extremely thin, it does suggest the possibility that a normal agenda item in Politburo meetings is the passage of CDs.

101. For documentation, see Lieberthal, Research Guide, pp. 188-89.

102. For details, see: Lieberthal, Research Guide, pp. 11-13, 238-48. Mao Tse-tung repeatedly resorted to this tactic during the mid-1950s when he found himself in opposition to much of the rest of the leadership on agricultural policy. "National conferences" convened on various subjects are also frequently used for this purpose. At other times, these conferences play a role in policy implementation.

103. Ibid., pp. 3-23.

104. Information and documentation on each of these are presented respectively in ibid., pp. 141-45, 179-81, 188-90, and 248-49.

105. See the reviews of these processes for May 1958—September 1959 and January—May 1966 in ibid., pp. 11-21.

106. For example, the Central Committee convened a meeting of provincial Party secretaries in charge of industry simultaneously with the latter stage of the 1958 Peitaiho Conference: Jen-min shou-ts'e (1959), p. 32. There is some indication that Liu Shao-ch'i might have used the 30 December 1964 Supreme State Conference to oppose Mao Tse-tung's ideas as articulated by the Party Chairman at a December 1964 Central Work Conference and embodied in the January 1965 "Twenty-three Points": Lieberthal, Research Guide, pp. 200-21.

107. See Lieberthal, Research Guide, passim.

108. See, especially, Ahn, Chinese Politics, pp. 84-184; and Parris Chang, Power and Policy in China (University Park, Pa.: Pennsylvania State University Press, 1975).

109. See JMJP, 30 June 1977--FBIS/PRC, 1 July 1977, E-6-15, and JMJP, 17 July 1977--FBIS/PRC, 18 July 1977, E-1-14, on, respectively, the "Outline Summary Report on the Work of the Academy of Sciences" and "On Certain Questions on Accelerating the Development of Industry." Confirmation that the "Outline Summary Report" was originally intended to be issued as a CD (albeit with the State Council joining the Central Committee as the issuing organ) is provided by Peking Review, 44 (28 October 1977): 5.

110. The drafting process for a number of major pre-1966 Central Documents can be reconstructed in some detail from the available data. Some of the most notable attempts to do this include: the 1957

decentralization decrees (Nicholas R. Lardy, "Central Control and Redistribution in China: Central-Provincial Fiscal Relations since 1949" [Ph.D. dissertation, The University of Michigan, 1975]); the Twelve-Year National Agriculture Program (Parris Chang, Power and Policy in China); the series of CDs on the Socialist Education Campaign (Baum and Teiwes, Ssu-ch'ing, pp. 11-48); and a range of other CDs of the early 1960s on literature and art, industry, and agriculture policy (Ahn, Chinese Politics).

111. Text of the latest available draft in Ming Pao (American edition), 6-12 July 1977 (a series of articles). Partial text of earlier draft available in: Ch'i Hsin, pp. 187-94--SPRCM, no. 926 (23 May 1977): 31-37. The Ming Pao text is translated in Appendix I.

112. Text of the first of two drafts in P'an Ku, no. 103 (1 April 1977)--SPRCM, no. 921 (25 April 1977): 18-37. The second draft evidently differed from the first primarily in its dropping the reference to the "three directives as the key link": JMJP, 7 July 1977.

113. Texts of the 22 August and 2 September drafts (for details, see the case study below) in, respectively, Ming Pao, 21-29 May 1977 (a series of articles), and Ch'i Hsin, pp. 159-84--translated in SPRCM, no. 926 (23 May 1977): 8-30 (subsequent page references to this text refer to the SPRCM translation). The 2 September text is presented in Appendix I.

114. There is a great deal of information available on the contents of "On the General Program for the Work of the Whole Party and the Country," but data on the specific drafting process remain too sparse to undertake the kind of detailed analysis presented below on the drafting of the other two documents. The basic sources for the "General Program" are Chai Ch'ing, "Read an Unpublished Manuscript," Hsüeh-hsi yü p'i-p'an, no. 4 (14 April 1976): 11-19--translated in SPRCM, no. 870 (10 May 1976): 1-15; "On the General Program for All Work of the Whole Party and the Whole Country," P'an Ku, no. 103 (1 April 1977)--SPRCM, no. 921 (25 April 1977): 18-37; Ch'i Hsin, pp. 134-58 (identical to P'an Ku text); and JMJP, 7 July 1977--FBIS/PRC, 8 July 1977, E-5-18.

115. I have spelled out in detail Teng's political strategy during 1975 and his use of these issues to cement ties to potential allies in my "Sino-Soviet Relations in the 1970's," Rand Report no. R-2150-NA, chapter 2. I have highlighted related dimensions of the politics of

this period in the following articles: "China in 1975: The Internal Political Scene," Problems of Communism (May-June 1975): 1-11; "Strategies of Conflict in China during 1975-76," Contemporary China (December 1976): 7-14; and "The Foreign Policy Debate in Peking As Seen Through the Allegorical Articles, 1973-76," China Quarterly, no. 71 (September 1977): 528-54.

116. See Chou En-lai's "Report on the Work of the Government" to the Fourth NPC--text in Peking Review, no. 4 (24 January 1975): 21-25.

117. JMJP, 30 June 1977--FBIS/PRC, 1 July 1977, E-7. See also Appendix II.

118. As noted earlier, the original impetus for new policies in some of these issue areas--including science and technology--preceded the January 1975 NPC meeting. See supra, pp. 40-41.

119. The timing and substance of this set of instructions is derived from the following: JMJP, 9 March 1977--FBIS/PRC, 17 March 1977, E-9, notes the July 1975 date and gives a sense of the thrust of the instructions; K'ang Li and Yen Feng mention Mao's "ten-point thesis" on work in science and technology: p. 20 (all future page references to this article, unless specified otherwise, are to the SPRCM translation of the article); and a reference to Mao's "recent" instructions in this sphere that was contained in a document written in August 1975: "Several Questions on the Work in Science and Technology," Ch'i Hsin, pp. 187-94--translated in SPRCM, no. 926 (23 May 1977): 31 (this document is hereafter abbreviated as "Several Questions" and all future page references refer to the translation).

120. For information on this military conference and the ensuing decisions, see Asahi Shimbun, 7 March 1976--FBIS, 9 March 1976, p. 4; Liberation Army Daily, 10 March 1977--FBIS/PRC, 23 March 1977, E-15-16; and Victor Zorza, "China's Scrutable Struggle," Washington Post, 11 April 1976, pp. C-1 and C-4. This same conference undoubtedly provided a major impetus toward the drafting of the key document on industry discussed below.

121. "Cheng-tun"--FBIS/PRC, 1 July 1977, E-7, mistranslates this term here and elsewhere as "consolidate."

122. The 18 July date is from K'ang Li and Yen Feng, p. 16; Hu Yao-pang's identity is from "Teng Hsiao-p'ing's Interpolated Remarks

When Listening to Hu Yao-pang's Summary Report" (hereafter cited as "Report Meeting"), Ch'i Hsin, pp. 194-200--translated in SPRCM, no. 926 (23 May 1977): 37-42 (all future page references are to the translation). The remarks attributed to Hu in this transcript match those attributed to the "capitalist roader" sent to the Academy of Sciences on 18 July--see K'ang Li and Yen Feng, pp. 22-23. The substance of the charge from the Central leadership is given in JMJP, 30 June 1977--FBIS/PRC, 1 July 1977, E-7.

123. "Several Questions," p. 31.

124. Mentioned in JMJP, 30 June 1977--FBIS/PRC, 1 July 1977, E-11.

125. Hu Ch'iao-mu's identity is slightly problematic. The radicals simply referred repeatedly to the key role played by the "theoretician on Teng's personal staff." Given this person's major role in the drafting process, as detailed below, he must have participated in the key 26 September 1975 hui-pao meeting on the "Outline Report." Only two known participants in that meeting could have served on Teng's personal staff, however, as all the rest held major positions in the government bureaucracy. The two are Hu Ch'iao-mu and Li Ch'ang (see the transcript: "Several Questions," pp. 38-39). Given Hu's background, I assume that he is in fact the mystery "theoretician." In 1968 Li had headed the Peking Foreign Languages College, No. 2. He was identified as a leading member of the Chinese Academy of Sciences in March 1977, at the same time that a Central Work Conference made special arrangements for the rehabilitation of Teng Hsiao-ping.

126. K'ang Li and Yen Feng, p. 17.

127. "Several Questions," pp. 31-37. That this is the text of the 17 August draft is clear from two pieces of evidence. First, the draft refers to the fact that the authors have been at the Academy of Sciences for nearly one month ("Several Questions," p. 31). Second, a textual comparison with the information provided in the subsequent radical critique of the 17 August draft makes clear that the radicals were referring to this text (critique in K'ang Li and Yen Feng, pp. 17-19).

128. K'ang Li and Yen Feng, p. 19. An interesting sidelight is provided by a subsequent charge in the Chinese media that Mao had made this statement to one of the radicals. He, in turn, passed it on to the Liang Hsiao writing group, which immediately whipped up a

political furor over it. The radicals would not, however, give a copy of the full text of Mao's remarks to the moderates. Is it possible, then, that Teng began to try to protect himself against a threat the precise dimensions of which he could not calculate?

129. K'ang Li and Yen Feng, p. 19.

130. See, for example, JMJP, 9 March 1977--FBIS/PRC, 17 March 1977, E-7-13.

131. JMJP, 30 June 1977--FBIS/PRC, 1 July 1977, E-7-15.

132. The article by K'ang Li and Yen Feng provides a great deal of information on the drafting process. Also, the available partial text of the first draft of the "Outline Report" (i.e., "Several Questions," pp. 31-37) conforms to the description of the appendix on the "Outline Report" contained in a booklet printed and circulated by the radicals in August 1976: JMJP, 7 July 1977--FBIS/PRC, 8 July 1977, E-5.

133. Peking Review, no. 16 (15 April 1977): 24.

134. From the entries for Hua Kuo-feng in Appearances and Activities of Leading Personalities of the People's Republic of China, 1 January-31 December 1975.

135. Articles giving Hua Kuo-feng a central role in drafting the "Outline Report" from the start include: Peking Review, no. 44 (28 October 1977): 5; and Kirin Radio, 28 September 1977--FBIS/PRC, 5 October 1977, L-3.

136. JMJP, 9 March 1977--FBIS/PRC, 17 March 1977, E-12.

137. There is, of course, an alternative possibility--i.e., that Hua Kuo-feng was trying to undercut Teng's efforts in this sphere, perhaps at the behest of an increasingly suspicious Mao Tse-tung. There is a great deal of evidence to suggest that this was not the case and that Hua in fact worked closely and harmoniously with Teng during this period. For a detailed analysis, see Lieberthal, "Sino-Soviet Relations in the 1970's," chapter 2. Additionally, the radicals who opposed Teng's efforts also attacked Hua's August forum, as detailed below.

138. K'ang Li and Yen Feng, pp. 20, 22. The text of this revised draft is translated, _sans_ appendix, in Appendix I below. This text shows that the six articles in the 17 August revision were reduced to five articles in the revision. It also embodies the other changes mentioned in K'ang Li and Yen Feng.

139. The participation of Hua, Teng, and Yeh is derived from _JMJP_, 30 June 1977--_FBIS/PRC_, 1 July 1977, E-8. The events described on this page in _FBIS/PRC_ clearly took place at the September State Council meeting noted in _JMJP_, 9 March 1977--_FBIS/PRC_, 17 March 1977, E-7-8. It is not clear, however, from the available data whether this conference met before or after the 26 September 1975 _hui-pao_ meeting described below. I am assuming it met before, in part because at the end of the latter meeting Teng Hsiao-p'ing did not instruct his colleagues to present the report to the State Council.

140. _JMJP_, 30 June 1977--_FBIS/PRC_, 1 July 1977, E-8; _Peking Review_, no. 44 (28 October 1977): 5.

141. A partial text of the transcript of this meeting is available in "Report Meeting," pp. 37-42. It is clear that more has been left out of this text than meets the eye. For instance, quotations from this meeting presented in K'ang Li and Yen Feng, p. 22 ff., indicate that even some of Teng Hsiao-p'ing's comments at the meeting are missing from the available text. The authenticity of the parts of this text that are available, however, is demonstrated by the fact that both the radicals (in K'ang Li and Yen Feng, p. 22 ff.) and the moderates (in _JMJP_, 30 June 1977--_FBIS/PRC_, 1 July 1977, E-12) quote verbatim from remarks attributed in the text to Teng Hsiao-p'ing.

142. The available text, if it was originally circulated by the radicals, may omit Hua Kuo-feng's name because Hua could not be attacked at the time.

143. Unfortunately, information on the contents of _chung-fa_ (75) #9 is not available.

144. "Report Meeting," pp. 41-42.

145. Indeed, the radicals subsequently did argue that "the wind to reverse verdicts in educational circles was started in science and

technology": JMJP, 9 March 1977--FBIS/PRC, 17 March 1977, E-8. They also claimed that Chou Jung-hsin had, by 8 October, set up a drafting group to draft an "Outline Report" on education: K'ang Li and Yen Feng, p. 24.

146. JMJP, 30 June 1977--FBIS/PRC, 1 July 1977, E-7; Peking Review, no. 44 (28 October 1977): 5.

147. K'ang Li and Yen Feng, pp. 23-24.

148. Ibid., p. 27.

149. His identity is revealed by his authorship of the article "Teng Hsiao-p'ing's 'Reorganization' Is Precisely Restoration" in JMJP, 29 April 1976, p. 3. The Chinese media recently revealed that the person who authored this article was in fact the key partisan of the Gang of Four in the Academy of Sciences: JMJP, 30 June 1977--FBIS/PRC, 1 July 1977, E-9.

150. JMJP, 30 June 1977--FBIS/PRC, 1 July 1977, E-8.

151. JMJP, 9 March 1977--FBIS/PRC, 17 March 1977, E-12.

152. K'ang Li and Yen Feng, p. 17.

153. This paragraph combines information presented in JMJP, 9 March 1977--FBIS/PRC, 17 March 1977, E-8; and JMJP, 30 June 1977--FBIS/PRC, 1 July 1977, E-8. Note that the latter FBIS/PRC mistranslates the original Chinese and thus mistakenly states that the radicals produced "millions" of copies in Shanghai and distributed them "to the masses" (instead of "tens of thousands" of copies to the "basic levels").

154. JMJP, 30 June 1977--FBIS/PRC, 1 July 1977, E-8.

155. JMJP, 9 March 1977--FBIS/PRC, 17 March 1977, E-9.

156. Ibid.

157. Ibid.

158. Ibid., E-10.

159. Communicated in CD(76)#1, passed on 3 February 1976.

160. Reported in JMJP, 9 March 1977--FBIS/PRC, 17 March 1977, E-10. The article referred to must be "Strike Back at the Rightist Wind to Reverse Verdicts in Science and Technology Circles," Hung-ch'i, no. 2 (February 1976): 3-11.

161. Text of the 1966 "February Outline Report" is in CR Docs, pp. 3-12.

162. On Liu Chung-yang's action in March 1976, see JMJP, 30 June 1977--FBIS/PRC, 1 July 1977, E-8.

163. JMJP, 25 April 1976, p. 3.

164. Ibid., E-9.

165. This highlights the importance to a faction of being able to place people in each major functional system. The media now allege that it was Chang Ch'un-ch'iao who put Liu Chung-yang in the Academy of Sciences although the means by which Chang accomplished this are unclear. See ibid., E-8. It could be that, as one observer in the PRC related to me in August 1977, Chang had Politburo level responsibility for educational policy in 1975. Chang's responsibility for the educational realm is strongly suggested in an article on the overthrow of Chou Jung-hsin in JMJP, 15 September 1977--FBIS/PRC, 16 September 1977, E-12. Perhaps Chang's involvement in educational affairs permitted him to appoint one key person to the Academy of Sciences. Unfortunately, we know too little about the power of appointment in the PRC to draw any conclusions with confidence.

166. The battle over this document still raged at least as late as the summer of 1976: Chung Ko, "The Struggle around the Outline Report on Science and Technology," Peking Review, no. 44 (28 October 1977): 5 and 8.

167. The major sources for the drafting process on this document are: Kung Hsiao-wen, "Teng Hsiao-p'ing and the 'Twenty Articles,'" Hsüeh-hsi yü p'i-p'an, no. 6 (14 June 1976): 14-19--SPRCM, no. 879 (12 July 1976): 1-10; the summary of Teng Hsiao-p'ing's comments at a hui-pao meeting on 18 August 1976 as reported in Ch'i Hsin, pp. 184-86--SPRCM, no. 926 (3 May 1977): 28-30; JMJP, 17 July 1977, pp. 1-3; and the texts of two drafts of this document (rationale for dating them is presented below): the 22 August 1975 draft in Ming Pao, 21-29 May 1977 (a series of articles); and the 2 September 1975 draft in Ch'i Hsin, pp. 159-84--SPRCM, no. 926 (23 May

1977): 8-28. All page references to materials that have been translated refer to the translations rather than the originals. It is likely that the 2 September 1975 draft in SPRCM no. 926 originated in one of three booklets published by the radicals in Shanghai in August 1976 If so, the media now claim that this text "was not based on the original copy but on a handwritten copy riddled with errors": JMJP, 7 July 1977--FBIS/PRC, 8 July 1977, E-5 (this FBIS/PRC translation erroneously translates the original Chinese as saying that the radicals put out only one booklet). A translation of the 2 September text is given in Appendix I.

168. This statement, often made in the Chinese media, is dramatically illustrated by the figures on gross value of industrial output contained in Robert Field, Nicholas Lardy and John Emerson, Provincial Industrial Output in the People's Republic of China: 1949-1975 (Foreign Economic Report No. 12, U.S. Department of Commerce, September 1976), pp. 10-11, 17, et passim.

169. It was probably at one of these conferences that Teng Hsiao-p'ing made his 5 March 1975 speech that castigated the situation since the Cultural Revolution, ridiculed the current radical-inspired campaign on bourgeois rights, and called for devising and implementing a set of rational rules and regulations in order to achieve the four modernizations: mentioned in Kung Hsiao-wen, p. 2.

170. JMJP, 16 July 1977. See Appendix II for the available Central Documents from this period.

171. Ibid.

172. Kung Hsiao-wen, pp. 1-2.

173. NCNA English, 16 and 18 August--carried in FBIS/PRC, nos. 160 and 161 (1975) respectively.

174. See the partial summary of Teng's remarks at this meeting in SPRCM, no. 926 (23 May 1977): pp. 28-30.

175. Kung Hsiao-wen, pp. 1, 3.

176. Ming Pao, 21-29 May 1977.

177. Kung Hsiao-wen specifies these articles as having grown directly out of Teng's comments at the 18 August meeting although Kung

mistakenly states that these articles first appeared in the 2 September draft: Kung Hsiao-wen, pp. 4-6.

178. JMJP, 16 July 1977. This source claims that Yao Wen-yuan learned the details of the results of this review in September, suggesting that the review itself might have taken place in August. An alternative explanation is given below.

179. Text of the 2 September draft is presented in Appendix I. The date is given in the text. Note the caveats about this draft mentioned in note 153 above.

180. The article on rectification of management, for instance, was revised and moved from Article 12 to Article 4.

181. JMJP, 16 July 1977.

182. Ibid.

183. Ibid.

184. Kung Hsiao-wen, p. 6, simply says the draft was given to the "theoretician" on Teng's staff. I have identified this "theoretician" as Hu Ch'iao-mu according to the line of reasoning spelled out above in the section on the "Outline Report."

185. JMJP, 16 July 1977; Peking Review, no. 42 (14 October 1977): 7.

186. Kung Hsiao-wen, pp. 7-8. Kung also mistakenly asserts that it was only in this 25 October draft that the reference to the "three directives as the key link" was removed, again suggesting the limitations on the radicals' access to documents in this sphere.

187. Ibid.

188. JMJP, 16 July 1977; Peking Review, no. 42 (14 October 1977): 12.

189. Kung Hsiao-wen, p. 9.

190. Details in JMJP, 16 July 1977.

191. Interestingly, the "Twenty-three Points" is one of the extremely few pre-Cultural Revolution Central Documents for which we have listed the chu-sung chi-kuan, and the list for this major document

excludes the military. Is the inclusion of the military in Party groups on the CD routing, then, primarily a Cultural Revolution-generated phenomenon?

192. Kau, p. 78. For a similar list on another CD, see the text of CD (74) #21 in Issues and Studies 11, no. 1 (January 1975): 101-2.

193. Text in CR Docs, pp. 377-78.

194. See the texts cited in notes 192 and 193.

195. See Oksenberg, "Communications," pp. 12-15, for additional information on "transmission meetings."

196. One informant commented that in his unit such requests were often made rather rudely after the Cultural Revolution. A person would say, for instance, "Your p'u-t'ung-hua is so bad that I could not understand what you said. Please reread the document."

197. Partial text in Kau, pp. 78-95. This CD was issued on 13 January 1972.

198. Oksenberg reports that such cynicism was in fact a serious problem in: "Communications," p. 13.

199. Text of Wang's speech is given in Chinese Law and Government 7, no. 3 (Fall 1974): 7-32.

200. Ibid., p. 7.

201. Ibid., p. 16.

202. Actually, Chou had been the political commissar for the Kunming Military Region (MR) at the outset of the Cultural Revolution and was identified as a "responsible person" of the MR in 1972. I am assuming that he in fact retained his position as political commissar.

203. Chinese Law and Government 7, no. 3 (Fall 1974): 8.

204. Ibid., p. 10.

205. For a summary of these opinions, see ibid., pp. 15-17.

206. Ibid., pp. 20, 26-27.

207. The available copy of the "Twenty-three Points," for instance, was printed by the Fukien Provincial Party Committee--Baum and Teiwes, p. 118.

208. Kiangsi Radio, 18 July 1974--FBIS/PRC, 23 July 1974, G-4. This CD was issued on 1 July 1974.

209. Szechwan Radio, 14 July 1974--FBIS/PRC, 15 July 1974, J-1-2.

210. Yunnan Radio, 6 July 1974--FBIS/PRC, 8 July 1974, J-4-5.

211. Kiangsu Radio, 9 July 1974--FBIS/PRC, 11 July 1974, G-1-3.

212. Honan Radio, 12 July 1974--FBIS/PRC, 17 July 1974, H-1.

213. Heilungkiang Radio, 14 July 1974--FBIS/PRC, 18 July 1974, L-1-3.

214. If the reference materials being circulated with the CD include pictures or graphics of some sort, as was the case with CD (72) #24 on the Lin Piao affair (text in Kau, pp. 96-105), then these visual materials are circulated among the participants in the study group but the text is not, according to this informant. The same informant commented that a senior cadre in his study group would occasionally simply reach over and take a document off the table to peruse during discussion. Lower ranking cadres would not dare to take such liberties.

215. Chinese Government and Law 7, no. 3 (Fall 1974): 26-27.

216. Ibid., p. 15.

217. Oksenberg covers variations of this in his "Communications," pp. 12-14.

218. The National Conference convened from 8 February to 31 March 1963. Documentation on this conference and on the preceding Tenth Plenum is provided in Lieberthal, Research Guide, pp. 198-99 and 191-93 respectively.

219. Texts in Issues and Studies 11, no. 1 (January 1975): 101-4; Chung-kung yen-chiu 8, no. 12: 6/20-6/21.

220. More precisely, to: Party committees at various provinces, (directly administered) municipalities, and autonomous regions;

Party committees at various military regions, provincial military districts and field armies; Military Affairs Commission; Party committees at various general headquarters of armed services, various arms and branches; and the leadership groups and core groups of the departments of the Central Committee and of the ministries and commissions of the State Council.

221. Actually, to both the counties and the regiment level in the PLA.

222. These dates should be understood, of course, to indicate the latest time by which second tier dissemination began in each province. For the provinces where information on second tier dissemination of CD (74) #21 appeared in the media, the dates for the earliest evidence of this dissemination are as follows:

Province	Date of earliest second tier dissemination mentioned	Date of provincial radio broadcast	FBIS/PRC (date and pages)
Yunnan	5 July	6 July	8 July, J-4-5
Chekiang	5 July	8 July	10 July, G-1-4
Kirin	6 July	7 July	8 July, L-2-4
Szechwan	8 July	14 July	15 July, J-1-2
Kiangsu	8 July (approx)	9 July	11 July, G-1-3
Shanghai	8 July	10 July	11 July, G-4-6
IMAR	9 July	10 July	11 July, K-1-3
Kweichow	10 July	10 July	15 July, J-2-3
Kwangtung	10 July	12 July*	15 July, H-4-5
Anhwei	10 July	10 July	17 July, G-1-3
Honan	11 July (approx)	12 July	17 July, H-1-2
Heilungkiang	12 July	14 July	18 July, L-1-4
Hunan	14 July (approx)	15 July	16 July, H-1-4
Tsinghai	15 July	15 July	19 July, M-1-2
Kiangsi	18 July (approx)	18 July	23 July, G-4
Hupeh	18 July (approx)	18 July	23 July, H-7-8
Shensi	27 July	29 July	30 July, M-1-3
Shantung	28 July	28 July	31 July, G-6-7
Sinkiang	4 August	4 August	7 August, M-3-[illegible]

*Canton City Broadcast

223. This is strongly suggested by the fact that broadcasts from a few provinces in June 1974--i.e., during the month before CD (74) #21 was issued--clearly and concretely anticipated the contents of this

document. See, for example, Canton Radio, 21 June 1974--FBIS/PRC, 26 June 1974, H–4-5.

224. Yunnan Radio, 6 July 1974--FBIS/PRC, 8 July 1974, J–4-5; ibid., 10 July 1974--FBIS/PRC, 11 July 1974, J-1.

225. Szechwan Service, 28 July 1974--FBIS/PRC, 29 July 1974, J–1-2. This conference convened from 15 to 25 July in Chungking and attracted participants from all over the province.

226. Szechwan Radio, 19 July 1974--FBIS/PRC, 22 July 1974, J–1-2.

227. FBIS/PRC, 23 July 1974, J–1-3.

228. Kiangsu Radio, 9 July 1974--FBIS/PRC, 11 July 1974, G–1-3.

229. Kiangsu Radio, 24 July 1974--FBIS/PRC, 25 July 1974, G–10-11.

230. Kiangsu Radio, 15 July 1974--FBIS/PRC, 18 July 1974, G–5-7. The broadcast does not give the date of the editorial, but usual practice is to broadcast an editorial within one day of its publication in the paper.

231. Kweichow Radio, 22 August 1974--FBIS/PRC, 27 August 1974, J–1-2.

232. Shantung Radio, 18 August 1974--FBIS/PRC, 21 August 1974, G–7-9.

233. Kiangsi Radio, 20 August 1974--FBIS/PRC, 23 August 1974, G–1-2.

234. Ibid., G–3-4.

235. Kirin Radio, 28 July 1974--FBIS/PRC, 30 July 1974, L–5-8. The conference convened from 15 to 22 July.

236. Hupeh Radio, 18 July 1974--FBIS/PRC, 23 July 1974, H–7-8.

237. Szechwan Radio, 28 July 1974--FBIS/PRC, 29 July 1974, J–1-2.

238. Kiangsu Radio, 24 July 1974--FBIS/PRC, 25 July 1974, G–10-11.

239. Kweichow Radio, 23 July 1974--FBIS/PRC, 25 July 1974, J-1.

240. Szechwan Radio, 19 July 1974--FBIS/PRC, 22 July 1974, J-1-2.

241. Yunnan Radio, 9 July 1974--FBIS/PRC, 11 July 1974, J-1.

242. Szechwan Radio, 19 July 1974--FBIS/PRC, 22 July 1974, J-1-2.

243. IMAR Radio, 10 July 1974--FBIS/PRC, 11 July 1974, J-1; Chekiang Radio, 11 July 1974--FBIS/PRC, 16 July 1974, G-1-4; Anhwei Radio, 15 July 1974--FBIS/PRC, 17 July 1974, G-1-3.

244. Yunnan Radio, 9 July 1974--FBIS/PRC, 11 July 1974, J-1.

245. Canton Radio, 12 July 1974--FBIS/PRC, 15 July 1974, H-4-5.

246. Hupeh Radio, 26 July 1974--FBIS/PRC, 29 July 1974, H-1-2.

247. See, for example, the editorials in: Inner Mongolia Daily, 10 July 1974--FBIS/PRC, 11 July 1974, K-4-5; Fukien Daily, 11 July 1974--FBIS/PRC, 12 July 1974, G-5; Tachung Daily (Shantung)--FBIS/PRC 19 July 1974, G-7-9; and Szechwan Daily, 22 July 1974--FBIS/PRC, 23 July 1974, J-1-3.

248. Szechwan Radio, 14 July 1974--FBIS/PRC, 15 July 1974, J-2. Emphasis added.

249. Article 1. Emphasis added.

250. Szechwan Radio, 14 July 1977--FBIS/PRC, 15 July 1977, J-1. Emphasis added.

251. If the FBIS/PRC translation is accurate.

252. Szechwan Radio, 14 July 1977--FBIS/PRC, 15 July 1977, J-1.

253. Yunnan Radio, 6 July 1974--FBIS/PRC, 8 July 1974, J-4-5.

254. Chekiang Radio, 8 July 1974--FBIS/PRC, 10 July 1974, G-1.

255. Ibid., G-2.

256. Chekiang Radio, 8 July 1974--FBIS/PRC, 10 July 1974, G-1.

257. Ten years earlier Liu Shao-ch'i purportedly used a similar tactic to blur the differences between Mao's "Ten Points" and Liu's

"Revised Later Ten Points" by lumping them together and referring to them as the "Double Ten Points"; see Authority, Participation and Cultural Change in China, ed. Stuart Schram (Cambridge: Cambridge University Press, 1973), p. 79.

258. For another instance of the use of this ploy in the transmission of CD (74) #21, see, for example, Shanghai Radio, 10 July 1974--FBIS/PRC, 11 July 1974, G-4-6.

259. Hunan Radio, 14 July 1974--FBIS/PRC, 16 July 1974, H-1-4.

260. Text of translation in SPRCP, nos. 5648-5652 (8-12 July 1974), pp. 217-19.

261. These, of course, are simplifications of the titles of these documents. The documents themselves were issued, respectively, on 20 May 1963, September 1963, 10 September 1964, and 18 January 1965. Texts are available in Baum and Teiwes, pp. 58-94 and 102-26. I am indebted to Richard Baum for providing me with the original Chinese copies of several of these texts.

262. On the differences among these and the political disputes over them, see Baum and Teiwes, pp. 11-48; and Baum, Prelude, passim.

263. That this was by no means merely a reflection of JMJP's treatment of the Socialist Education Campaign CDs is proven by similar research conducted on other major documents of the pre-1966 period. Two examples will suffice, each presented in the tabular form used in the text for the SEC documents:

Document	JMJP Editorial Date	Article Number in the CD Reflected in the Editorial
"Regulations on the Work of Rural People's Communes" (draft)*	25 November 1960	26
	21 December 1960	2
	29 December 1960	20
	12 January 1961	27
	20 January 1961	15, 25
	23 January 1961	10
	27 January 1961	4
	2 April 1961	1, 2, 10, 16, 20, 27, 33, 55, 57
	6 May 1961	49
	21 June 1961	6, 27, 36-39

Document	JMJP Editorial Date	Article Number in the CD Reflected in the Editorial
"Seventy Articles on Industry"**	22 July 1961	42
	8 August 1961	2
	6 September 1961	34, 35
	17 December 1961	37-47
	24 December 1961	9
	12 January 1962	1

* Issued in May 1961. Chinese text available in the Asia Library at The University of Michigan. This text was itself a revision of an earlier twelve-article version.

**For summary of text, see CC Docs, pp. 689-94. Date of issue is uncertain.

264. See the list in Appendix II.

265. Peking Review, no. 44 (28 October 1977): 19.

266. See the list in Appendix II.

267. Texts are in, respectively, the following FBIS/PRC: 11 July 1974, K–4-5; 12 July 1974, G-5; 19 July 1974, G–7-9; 18 July 1974, G–5-7; 16 July 1974, H–4-5; 22 July 1974, J–1-3; 31 July 1974, L–4-6; 19 August 1974, M–4-5; 22 August 1974, J–1-3. This clearly need not exhaust the list of provincial editorials reflecting this CD. Others may have been published but not broadcasted or were broadcasted but not translated in FBIS/PRC. Also, the search in FBIS/PRC for these carried only through the end of August 1974, and it is possible that more editorials appeared in September and later. This list is, therefore, illustrative rather than definitive.

268. P'eng Teh-huai at the Lushan Conference in July 1959 evidently complained that this had been the case in policy making during the previous months. See his comments to the Northwest Group as documented in Lieberthal, Research Guide, p. 142.

269. Unless, of course, the issue under scrutiny is one that by its very nature cuts across a range of functional areas.

270. Oksenberg, "Arena," pp. 392-94, discusses several dimensions of this strategy.

271. Obviously the degree of harm to the system _during_ the Cultural Revolution itself was far greater.

272. For a list of the new Politburo elected by their plenums, see: NCNA, 20 August 1977--_FBIS/PRC_, 22 August 1977, E-1.

273. See, for instance, _JMJP_, 17 March 1977--_FBIS/PRC_, 31 March 1977, E-3.

274. For example, Chou En-lai managed to make Chou Jung-hsin, who was clearly a moderate, the Minister of Education in 1975, when Chang Ch'un-ch'iao evidently held responsibility for the educational system in the Politburo. That Chang held responsibility for the educational system at this time is suggested by: _JMJP_, 15 September 1977--_FBIS/PRC_, 16 September 1977, E-12; _JMJP_, 23 October 1977--_FBIS/PRC_, 26 October 1977, E-4.

275. Mao often used a variety of methods to circumvent normal bureaucratic channels in communicating with lower levels in the hierarchy. These included inspection tours during which he met face-to-face with local leaders, personal correspondence with officials at various levels in the political system, and meetings he could convene that would be attended by a group selected by the Chairman. While Mao evidently enjoyed "legitimate access" to almost any issue area, he sometimes moved boldly to thrust an issue of concern into the "campaign" arena, where he could have greater influence over it than would normally be the case. This was, for instance, a persistent tactic Mao used in dealing with issues in health policy, as documented by David M. Lampton, _The Politics of Medicine in China_ (Boulder: Westview Press, 1977). Mao also "planted" loyal followers in units controlled by people whom he regarded with distrust. In his discussion of the tactics he had adopted to whittle down Lin Piao's power during 1970-71, for instance, Mao called this ploy "mixing sand": Kau, p. 62.

276. This is reflected in the new Party Constitution passed in August 1977, the first sentence of Article 11 of which states, "Party committees on all levels operate on the principle of combining collective leadership with individual responsibility under a division of labor." See: NCNA, 23 August 1977--_FBIS/PRC_, Supplement No. 9, 1 September 1977, p. 68.

GLOSSARY OF CHINESE TERMS

ch'ao-sung chi-kuan	抄送机关
cheng-tun	整顿
chi-mi	机密
chih-shih	指示
ching-shen	精神
chou	州
chu-sung chi-kuan	主送机关
ch'uan-ta	传达
ch'uan-ta hui-i	传达会议
chüeh-mi	决密
chüeh-ting	决定
chung-fa	中发
ch'ung-fen	充分
fang-sheng hsüeh	仿生学
fen-kung chih-tu	分工制度

hsien	县
hui-pao	汇报
hui-pao hui-i	汇报会议
i-chien	意见
kuei-k'ou	归口
kuei-ting	规定
k'ung-tung-ti	空洞地
mi-chien	密件
ming-ling	命令
p'i-fa jen	批发人
p'i-Lin p'i-K'ung	批林批孔
pien-hao	编号
p'u-tung hua	普通话
shen-p'i jen	审批人
ts'ao-an	草案
tuan-p'ing	短评
t'ung-chih	通知
t'ung-ling	通令
t'ung-pao	通报
yuan-chien	元件

APPENDIX I

Some Questions on Accelerating the Development of Industry

(Discussion draft, Sept. 2, 1975)*

Table of Contents

---

*"Kuan-yü chia-k'uai fa-chan kung-yeh ti jo-kan wen-t'i." Source: Ch'i Hsin, Ssu-jen-pang shih-chien t'an-so (Hong Kong: Ch'i shih nien tai tsa-chih she, April 1977), pp. 159-84. This translation originally appeared in SPRCM, no. 926 (May 23, 1977): 8-28. I have checked this translation against the Chinese text and have made some editorial and minor substantive changes.

Acting on Chairman Mao's instructions, the Second Plenary Session of the 10th Party Central Committee and the Fourth National People's Congress proposed a grand task for the development of the national economy of our country in the coming 25 years. The first step is to build an independent and relatively complete industrial system and national economic system before the year 1980; the second step is to achieve overall modernization of agriculture, industry, national defense, and science and technology before the end of this century, so that our national economy will march in the front ranks of the world. The next ten years are crucial years for the achievement of the above-mentioned two step idea, and we must, under the guidance of Chairman Mao's revolutionary line, redouble our efforts to bring about a new flying leap in the national economy.

Socialist industry is the leading force of our national economy. It is only by accelerating the development of industry that we can powerfully support agriculture and push forward the development of the national economy as a whole; effectively strengthen national defense and make good preparations against wars of aggression; and further strengthen the material foundation of the dictatorship of the proletariat and better support the revolutionary struggles of the people of the world. At present international factors of both revolution and war are growing. A world war will break out one day. The Soviet revisionists' strategic emphasis is placed in Europe, but they always want to attack us. In the time that we have won, we must work intensely and realistically and must not let this time waste away. The question of the speed of industrial development is a major and sharp political question. While striving to develop agriculture, the whole Party and the people of the whole country must struggle to speed up the development of industry.

1. The General Work Program

Chairman Mao's directives on studying theory to oppose and prevent revisionism, stability and unity, and pushing the national economy forward are the general program for all kinds of work of the whole Party, the whole Army and the whole country. To accelerate the development of industry, we must take a firm grasp of this general program.

On the industrial front the struggle between the two classes, two roads and two lines is extremely fierce. New and old bourgeois elements collaborate with one another; they commit graft and theft, indulge in profiteering, and wildly attack socialism. In a small number of enterprises capitalist tendencies are serious; they disrupt state plans and are engaged in illegal activities of producing on their own and exchanging [material and goods] on their own. The bourgeois style of life has occurred among a number of Party members, a number of cadres and a number of workers. The leadership of some enterprises is not in the hands of genuine Marxists and the worker masses.

Some comrades are indifferent to this situation. Although they too pay lip service to the Party's basic line, they in fact put aside the struggle between the two classes and two roads instead of grasping this principal contradiction. [They follow a policy of] you attack me and I attack you without end. A small number of leaders who carry out bourgeois factional activities vie for power and profit, setting up mountain strongholds and creating a split. They upset things so that the enterprises have no peace, the localities have no peace, and the Party has no peace. The class enemies take the opportunity to fish in troubled water and have a good grab, with some even usurping the power of leadership. Returning to the past under the banner of opposing returning to the past and promoting restoration under the banner of opposing restoration, they undermine revolution and production. Good cadres of the Party, advanced model people and advanced collectives are kicked off the stage. While bad people dominate, good people suffer. In these places and in these enterprises management is chaotic, production has long been stagnant, and in some cases degeneration has set in.

All regions, departments and enterprises must carry out Chairman Mao's three directives in a penetrating, all-round and sustained manner. They must organize the cadres and the masses to read conscientiously, to make clear, in the light of reality, the question of strengthening the dictatorship of the proletariat, and to use the Marxist stand, viewpoint and method to analyze the complicated conditions of the current class struggle. They must uncover the essence through the appearance and strictly distinguish between and correctly handle the two different types of contradictions. They must stick to the Party's basic line and criticize the revisionist line, capitalist tendencies and bourgeois factionalism. They must resolutely strike at the wrecking activities of the class enemies. They must pay attention to carrying out well the work of rectification in industry, and adopt practical and effective measures to resolve certain problems of confusion and laxity in industrial and enterprise management. They must unfold in depth the mass movement to learn from Tach'ing in industry and move production and construction forward.

Chairman Mao's three important directives are closely interrelated; they are an integral whole. To carry out these three directives is to carry out the Party's basic line, the Party's general line for socialist construction, and the Party's line of unity and victory. It is necessary to give first place to doing a good job of studying the theory of proletarian dictatorship, promote stability and unity and promote the development of production. If we pay attention only to production but forget about the struggle between the two classes and two roads, we shall make a bungle of our work, let alone socialist construction. It is also impermissible to pay no attention to production, to make no effort to increase production, and to put production in a non-essential or insignificant position. Without powerful development of social productive forces, the socialist system cannot be fully consolidated. Under no circumstances must we criticize doing well at production under the command of revolution as [a manifestation of] the "theory of productive forces" and "putting vocational work in command." We must carry out the policy of "grasping revolution, promoting production, promoting work, and promoting preparedness against war" in all of our work and achieve conspicuous results.

2. Party Leadership

The key to whether or not we can consciously and thoroughly implement Chairman Mao's three important directives depends on the Party's leadership.

With regard to the leadership of Party committees in the enterprises at present, there are roughly [the following] four conditions:

1. [Party committees which are] resolute in carrying out the Party's basic line, principles and policies, dare to lead and accept responsibility, unite together, and grasp well both revolution and production.

2. [Party committees whose] leading groups are confronted, in varying degrees, with "soft, lax, and lazy" problems. Some of the leaders of these units put "fear" to the fore; they dare not uphold principles, dare not commend the good and dare not criticize the bad. This puts the Party organization in a feeble and weak position. In other cases, they are torn by disunity and practice bourgeois factionalism, with each blowing his own horn or singing his own tunes; they are

incapable of forming a nucleus. Some whose revolutionary will has declined muddle along, take a long rest for a minor illness or groan without illness; they follow the beaten track in their work and are incompetent.

3. Power is held by unreformed petty intellectuals and "brave elements." These people are ignorant politically and totally inexperienced in production, and yet, criticizing and gesticulating, they are intent on correcting others. Singing only high tunes, they do nothing practical. They at random put the hats of "returning to the past," "practicing retrogression," "being conservative forces," and "pulling carts only without looking at the road" on others. This restrains the activism of the broad cadres and the masses.

4. Power is held by bad people. Some are grafters, thieves, speculators and profiteers, and some are anti-Party, anti-socialist rightists. Abusing their power, they perpetrate every misdeed. On the one hand, they woo and corrupt a section of people and cultivate their own influence; on the other hand, they attack and falsely accuse good revolutionary cadres and workers, exercise bourgeois dictatorship, and promote restoration and regression.

People in the third and fourth categories are a minority, but they do great harm. The fact that the serious situation in these units has remained unchanged for a long time is because they have behind-the-scenes backing.

To rectify enterprises, it is first of all necessary to rectify the Party's leadership. Party committees of various departments, provinces, municipalities and autonomous regions must undertake analysis of all enterprises under them one by one. In the light of different conditions and by separate stages they should make a success, in about a year's time, of rectifying the leading groups of all enterprises, including enterprises owned by the whole people and those operated under the system of collective ownership. They should first take care of key enterprises with a bearing on the whole situation and then enterprises in general. It is especially important to assign good No. 1 and No. 2 leaders to enterprise Party committees, comrades who have a high Party spirit and a good style of work and are capable of uniting with others.

Through rectification, those "soft, lax, and lazy" leading groups must be changed. Leading groups dominated by unreformed petty intellectuals and "brave elements" must be adjusted, so that power seized by bad people will be recaptured and leadership placed in the hands of genuine Marxists and the worker masses.

All enterprises must implement the principle of three-in-one combination of the old, the middle-aged and the young, and establish an efficient and not swollen and overstaffed, firm and powerful and not lax and weak, tough and not fragile leading group. Enterprises are in the front line of the battle, and all leading cadres must be capable of going to the front to direct the fight. Leading cadres who are experienced but are old and feeble may remain in the enterprises or go to the industrial leadership organs to serve as advisers.

All work and all political movements in the enterprises must be put under the unified leadership of the Party committees. Revolutionary committees, trade unions and Communist Youth League organizations must proceed with their work under the Party committee's unified leadership. No individual or organization will be allowed to rise above the Party committee, and it is necessary to struggle against erroneous tendencies to weaken the Party's leadership.

Party committees at the higher level must support the work of the Party committees of the enterprises.

3. Reliance on the Working Class

The question of who is relied on in running enterprises is one of class line.

Chairman Mao has pointed out long ago: "It is necessary to rely on the working class heart and soul." Currently, this is not being done in some localities and units. Instead of relying on the working class, they rely on this or that mountain stronghold. They make no class analysis but blindly follow the "rebels" and "elements going against the tide." As a result, they split the working-class ranks and divorce themselves from the vast worker masses.

Nine years have elapsed since the start of the great cultural revolution, and the worker masses are still divided into so-called conservative and rebelling factions. This is a mistake. We should differentiate the advanced, the intermediate and the backward on the basis of their actual performances in the socialist revolution and socialist construction.

We should take the advanced elements as the backbone, lead the intermediate ones forward, and help and educate the backward so as to strengthen unceasingly the revolutionary unity of the working-class ranks as a whole.

[We should] do a concrete analysis of rebelling and going against the tide. We must see which class is rebelled against and the nature of the tide that is being opposed. What is correct must be supported and what is incorrect must be criticized. What is reactionary must be stood up to, then investigated and criticized. In particular, we must be alert against a small number of bad people carrying out wrecking activities in the name of "rebelling" and "going against the tide." Leading cadres must stick to principles at all times. They must not bend with the wind, nor must they allow themselves to be bewitched by beautiful words or become so afraid of receiving a hat [political label] that they disarm themselves ideologically and even turn over their power to others.

A line of demarcation must be drawn between rebels and elements going against the tide on the one hand and advanced elements of the working class on the other. We cannot say that all those who have taken part in going against the tide or in rebelling are advanced elements of the working class. All those who, taking "rebelling" and "going against the tide" as capital, demand rewards from the Party and demand to join the Party and become officials must be turned down flatly. They must not only be turned down flatly, but must also be criticized.

We must wage a resolute struggle against bourgeois factionalism, exchanging blow for blow and not conceding an inch. Those who are still fomenting bourgeois factionalism are those who are in fact practicing revisionism and capitalism, and if they refuse to mend their ways despite repeated education they must be strictly dealt with. Party members are absolutely not permitted to engage in factional activities; those who persist in doing so must be expelled from the Party.

We must take concrete measures to ensure the fulfillment of the Party's policies. [We must] take off the [political] hats of all those workers, technicians, and cadres in general who have been branded as "conservatives" or as "standing on the wrong side," and the relevant dossier must be returned to the person concerned or destroyed. We must unite with over 95 percent of the cadres and the masses, mobilize all positive factors, and give full play to the drive, wisdom and creativeness of the worker masses so as to make a success of revolution and production in the enterprises.

4. Rectification of Enterprise Management

Since the Great Proletarian Cultural Revolution, many enterprises have adhered to the "Charter of the Anshan Iron and Steel Company," aroused the masses boldly, improved enterprise management, and enlivened all kinds of work. But still quite a portion of enterprises exist whose ideological and political work is weak, management chaotic, and labor productivity low. The quality of their products is bad, their consumption of raw materials is great, their production cost is high, and they are involved in many accidents, thereby inflicting heavy losses on the state and the people. These enterprises, while rectifying and strengthening their leading groups, must rectify their enterprise management and make their rules and regulations more strict.

We must not relax at all our effort to continue to criticize in depth the revisionist line on running enterprises. The aim of doing this is to strengthen, not weaken, the socialist enterprise management. Production control and rules and regulations are needed at all times, and will be needed even ten thousand years from now. The question is what line to follow and on whom we rely in enforcing them. Wholesale opposition to enterprise management and rules and regulations is bound to create a situation of anarchy. "Anarchy is incompatible with the interests and wishes of the people."

All enterprises must persevere in putting proletarian politics in command and ideological and political work first. It is essential to grasp well the building of primary Party branches and building of leading groups, to give play to the role of Party branches as fighting bastions and to the vanguard, exemplary role of Party members. Linking up with reality, it is necessary to make a success of the workers' theoretical study, of class education, of education in the current situation, and of education in revolutionary traditions. All political movements of the enterprises must proceed under the condition of maintaining production; production cannot be suspended to make revolution.

In all of its work, an enterprise must keep to the mass line, unfold mass movements on a large scale, and mobilize the masses boldly to do the work, instead of letting a small number of people handle things coolly and quietly. It must launch socialist labor competitions. Cadres at various levels in the enterprise must keep to the system of regular participation in collective productive labor and become one with the masses, instead of claiming that they are special. Workers must take part in the enterprise management. It is necessary to put into practice extensively the three-in-one combination of leading cadres, workers and technicians.

All enterprises must, under the unified leadership of their Party committees, set up an effective and independent production management command system, which will be responsible for managing and directing the daily production activities of the enterprises and for handling in time problems arising from production so as to insure that production is carried out normally. The Party committee should not handle directly all matters, big and small, lest it would be prevented from coming to grips with important things. It is necessary to establish efficient functional organs in accordance with the needs of production and the principle of simpler administration and better troops. These organs must be oriented to the masses, to the basic levels, and to the first line of production, and be closely coordinated with mass management in doing a good job of managing planning, technical work, labor, and financial work.

All enterprises must grasp the following principal economic and technical targets: (1) output target; (2) variety target; (3) quality target; (4) consumption target for raw materials, other materials, fuels and power; (5) labor productivity target; (6) cost of production target; (7) profit target; (8) target of ratio of working capital, and so on and so forth. Failing to achieve these targets and to fulfill the supply contracts according to the quality and quantity prescribed and according to the schedule laid down means failing to fulfill the state plans in an all-round manner, and where the state plans have not been fulfilled for a long time, the responsibility of the leadership must be investigated. All enterprises must consider it as a glory to have higher output, better quality, lower consumption of materials, and greater accumulation. They must consider it a disgrace to have lower output, poor quality, high consumption of materials, and to incur losses (outside losses permitted by policy). All those enterprises that have not reached their historically best level must make an effort to reach that level as soon as possible; while those which have must catch up with and surpass national and international advanced levels.

We must give first priority to quality, variety and standards. Products which are below the quality standard should not be allowed to leave the plant. Commodity departments and commercial departments have the right to refuse to purchase things that cannot be used. Where defective products have left the plant, [the enterprise concerned] must guarantee repair, replacements, and compensation.

Equal importance must be attached to production and economy. We must strive to reduce the consumption quotas for raw materials, fuels and power. Haste and leakages must be eliminated. Granaries must be checked, and warehouses investigated to reduce stockpiling and reduce losses through wear and tear. We must oppose extravagance and waste and cut down the non-productive expenditures. Financial departments have the right to refuse to pay for and underwrite spending items that do not conform to the financial system. Spending items that should not be included in the cost must not be so included. An enterprise has the right to resist unauthorized attempts to assign it tasks or to take away its products, funds, manpower, equipment and materials.

Labor organization must be improved, a good job must be done of the work of designating personnel assignments and setting labor quotas, and non-production personnel and personnel detached from production must be reduced. The utilization rate of work time must be raised, and activities which should be carried out during spare time may not be carried out during production time. At present some enterprises set up a large number of sports teams, cultural and art propaganda teams, militias and writing groups, and so forth which are detached from production, and have a great variety of other errands. This causes many young and able-bodied workers to be disengaged from the first line of production and causes the proportion of non-production personnel in the enterprises to rise to as high as 30-40 percent of the total work force. All these specialized teams that are detached from production must be disbanded. All personnel who should not be detached from production must return to production posts.

All enterprises must rely on the masses and, proceeding from actual needs, establish and strengthen the following principal production management systems: (1) a system of responsibility at each post [or: personal responsibility system]; (2) a system of checking attendance; (3) technical operating procedures; (4) a system of quality inspection; (5) a system of equipment management and maintenance; (6) a system of production safety; (7) a system of economic accounting, and so on and so forth. The specific content of these systems should be constantly changed and gradually perfected in accordance with changes in objective conditions. But these systems are essential and must be strictly enforced. Under no circumstances shall we permit any attempt to abolish or weaken these systems at will.

The system of [individual] responsibility is the core of an enterprise's rules and regulations. Without a strict system of responsibility, we can only fight for production in a chaotic manner. We must establish a system of responsibility and regard it as the key to rectifying enterprise management. Someone must assume responsibility for every piece of work and every position, and every cadre, every worker and every technician must have clearly defined duties. We must coordinate the [responsibility] system with mass movements properly, strengthen ideological and political work, and translate observance of rules and regulations into a conscious action of the masses.

5. Two Sources of Initiative

Since 1970, in carrying out the transformation of industrial management functions, an overwhelming majority of enterprises have been turned over to the management of local authorities, and the unified leadership of local Party committees over economic work has been strengthened. This has had marked effects on the development of industry and on the provision of support to agriculture from industry. The facts have entirely proven that "having two sources of initiative is much better than having one." We must persist in carrying out the work of reform of management functions.

Enterprises that should be turned over to local authorities must be so turned over. With the exception of trans-provincial and intercity railways, posts and telecommunications, navigation and shipping on the Yangtze River, civil aviation, oil transmission lines and ocean-going shipping as well as a small number of key enterprises and construction projects such as large oilfields and specialized construction teams which must be run primarily by the concerned ministries of the central government, all other enterprises, business units and construction units which have not been turned over to local authorities or are still run by the central ministries on behalf of the local authorities should be gradually turned over to the local authorities in the light of prevailing conditions or, alternatively, be subjected to a dual leadership by central and local authorities, with the main emphasis on local control.

Local Party committees must strengthen their leadership over industry. In principle, enterprises that are turned over to the local authorities by the central authorities and large and medium-sized enterprises originally under local administration are to be led and run by provincial, municipal and autonomous regional authorities and by authorities in cities that are directly under the provincial authorities.

They are principally to be led and administered by cities directly under the provinces and must not be "sent down" further. Now, the industrial management structure in many localities is not sound. They have an inadequate staff who are incapable of coping with the situation following decentralization. Many things are left unattended, the work of production supervision cannot be grasped, and the development of production has been adversely affected. In these localities it is necessary to establish and strengthen promptly the needed management machinery so as to do a really good job of production management.

The various concerned ministries of the Center must make a success of transfer and management of decentralized enterprises together with the local authorities, and must not wash their hands [of these enterprises]. Our present task is to build a nationwide industrial system and, moreover, to gradually build industrial systems in X [sic] cooperative zones. It is still impossible for various provinces and regions to form their own systems. For this reason, in the case of those large enterprises which bear on the overall national economy and which are subject to dual leadership with main emphasis on local control, the relevant departments of the Center must not only manage the principles, policies and unified planning, but must also manage the allocation of products and the supply of vital commodities beyond the capability of local authorities. On the appointment of principal leading cadres in these enterprises, the local authorities must consult with the relevant central departments. The local authorities must first of all guarantee the fulfillment of the plans of these enterprises.

Turning enterprises over to local authorities and introducing management at separate levels must not be allowed to weaken the centralized and unified [leadership of the] central authorities. What should be centralized, must be centralized, not decentralized. The central authorities must exercise centralized leadership over (1) the principles and policies for the national economy; (2) the principal production targets for industry and agriculture; (3) capital construction investments and major construction projects; (4) distribution of important materials; (5) procurement and allocation of principal commodities; (6) state fiscal budget and currency issuance; (7) the number of newly added workers and the total payroll; and (8) pricing of major industrial and agricultural products. No region or department will be allowed to go its own way regarding these items. Now some regions and units, in disregard of the interests of the general situation and the unified stipulations of the central authorities, formulate their policies at will, contravene state plans, alter the production orientation of decentralized enterprises at random, cut off the original cooperative ties, fail to fulfill tasks assigned by the higher authorities, indiscriminately undertake capital construction projects and expand the scale of construction, and make unwarranted acquisition and use of materials and funds. It is impermissible to increase the number of staff and workers and to enlarge the total payroll at will or to change the commodity prices without authorization.

6. Unified Planning

To assure high-speed and proportionate development of industry and the national economy as a whole and to achieve the goals of struggle for the coming ten years, it is necessary to strengthen the unified planning of the state. Be they central or local units, units owned by the whole people or units owned collectively, their production, construction and all other principal economic activities, including labor, wages, materials and finances, must be scrutinized and balanced level by level and be incorporated into the unified plans of the state, so that the whole nation will be like a coordinated chess game. If we do not undertake unified planning or if we sabotage it, we can become blind and open the floodgates for capitalism. And the result will be to undermine and wreck the socialist economy. Enterprises under collective ownership must be given stronger leadership, their initiative brought into play, and their spontaneous tendencies prevented.

It is necessary to do well in achieving a comprehensive balance of the plan in accordance with the Party's line, principles and policies, in accordance with the tasks and direction of main attack for developing the national economy, and in the light of actual possibilities. Priority must be given to ordering well the proportionate relationship between agriculture, light industry and heavy industry, the proportionate relationship between the raw material industry and the processing industry, the proportionate relationship between accumulation and consumption, the proportionate relationship between economic construction and national defense construction, the proportionate relationship between materials and equipment needed for maintenance of production facilities and those for capital construction, the proportionate relationship between "bone" and "meat," and so on and so forth.

In formulating plans, we must fully mobilize the masses and extensively solicit the opinions of primary units. We should work out the national unified plan by the method of "from the bottom to the top, integrating the top and the bottom, placing main emphasis on the horizontal and combining the horizontal and the vertical" and by achieving a balance level by level.

The formulation of plans must have an objective basis and must be positive and reliable, leaving ample leeway.

Plans must be serious in nature. All departments, regions and enterprises must resolutely carry out the plans transmitted to them with the approval of the Center. We must oppose the erroneous practices of neglecting the general situation, not implementing the state plan, and doing whatever one wants to do. Adjustments of plans must be made in accordance with prescribed procedures and submitted to the higher-ups for approval.

Planning and statistical agencies at various levels must be reinforced and filled out. Planning and statistical work must be strengthened, and statistics must reflect the actual conditions. Deceptive and false reports must be opposed.

7. Agriculture As the Foundation

Agriculture is the foundation of the national economy. Substantial development of industry is impossible without substantial development of agriculture. All industrial departments must solidly establish the concept of taking agriculture as the foundation, render better service to agriculture and consolidate the worker-peasant alliance.

National economic plans, be they national or local, must resolutely support arrangements according to the order of agriculture, light industry and heavy industry, with agriculture put in first place. The more industry develops and the bigger the proportion of industry grows, the greater will be the need to attach major importance to agriculture. This is an important law that has been proved by positive and negative experiences.

All industrial departments must understand the needs of agriculture. They must take it as their own important task to support the modernization of agriculture and make the greatest effort possible to supply agriculture with machinery, chemical fertilizer, fuels, power, construction materials, and means of transport, etc., and to help peasants master modern science and technology. They must contribute to the basic realization of agricultural mechanization in 1980 and to a bigger increase in agricultural production. At the same time, they should actively increase the supply of light industrial goods to the countryside and expand the material exchanges between cities and the countryside.

Cities must lead the villages forward. Every industrial city must, according to its own strength, lead one to several counties forward, helping them develop agriculture, forestry, animal husbandry, sideline occupations and fisheries, establish small-scale industries, increase the incomes of communes and brigades, and improve supplies to the city. This must be incorporated into the plans of all industrial cities and also must be handled by specialized agencies.

Wherever conditions are suitable, industrial and mining enterprises must, like Tach'ing, carry out integration of industry and agriculture and of urban and rural areas, engage in agricultural and sideline production, and gradually raise the level of self-sufficiency in grain and subsidiary foodstuffs. Where there is no reclaimable land but there are nearby rural villages, it is permissible, under the unified leadership and arrangement of the local Party committee, to place one or two communes under the leadership of the enterprises to help them develop agricultural and sideline production and become a base for supplying vegetables, meat and other subsidiary foodstuffs to industrial and mining enterprises.

Education on the worker-peasant alliance must be given to the staff and workers so that they will take the initiative to improve their relations with the peasants.

8. Large-scale Battles to Open Up Mines

The present [most] acute problem of industry is that the raw materials, fuel and power industries lag behind the processing industry. Particularly the iron and steel industry lags behind, and in the iron and steel industry and the entire raw materials industry, mines are a weak link. To accelerate the development of industry, it is necessary resolutely to implement the principle of "taking steel as the key link" and take mining as the prime target of attack. "Developing the processing industry without raw materials is like cooking without rice."

. . . . . . [sic]

The leadership at various levels must put mine construction in an important position, send out able cadres to grasp the mines, concentrate superior forces and make an effort to solve the problems of extraction, dressing and sintering of iron ores. In regions rich in iron ore, independent mining companies should be established.

Machinery manufacturing departments must actively develop advanced and large-scale mining equipment, transport equipment and other mining machinery. At the same time, we may import some crucial advanced technology mining equipment.

We must carry out comprehensive exploitation and comprehensive utilization of mining resources, and oppose "mono-operations." Planning committees at various levels must take up this type of task.

Simultaneously with vigorously opening up mines, we must properly solve problems of smelting and processing and make corresponding arrangements for the development of other industrial departments.

9. Tapping Potential, Innovation, and Transformation

Our country's industry has already acquired quite a base and is widely distributed. . . . . [sic] The present task is to make full utilization of the existing industrial base and make it unceasingly develop and expand through technical innovation and technical transformation and through rational organization and division of work and cooperation. This will prove more economical than investing in new construction projects, and yield faster visible results and larger returns. From now on, the growth of industrial production should depend primarily on developing the role of existing enterprises, not on building new enterprises. This is an important principle that must be followed.

The masses must be boldly mobilized in all industries and trades, so that a people's war for tapping potential, innovation and transformation may be waged in existing enterprises. We must criticize the erroneous ideas and practices of being unwilling to utilize the existing base and make the effort to tap potentials and instead building new enterprises at random.

It is necessary to break the boundaries between industries and between regions so as to make a success of socialist cooperation. Competent industrial departments at various levels must earnestly take up this task.

We must promote the communist style, facilitate the work of others and keep the difficulties for ourselves. We must combat the erroneous tendency to regard the means of production that belong to the whole people as belonging to the department, to the region or to the enterprise and to prefer that equipment lie idle rather than undertake cooperative tasks. We must oppose the erroneous idea of doing everything on our own without seeking the aid of others for anything.

Innovation, transformation and organization of cooperation must be subject to overall planning, and leadership over them must be strengthened. The key emphasis should be placed on boosting the output of raw materials, fuels and products in short supply, on raising the level of complete sets and comprehensive utilization. Processing industries with surplus productive capacity must organize a number of enterprises to switch to production of products in short supply. Existing renewal and transformation funds must be included in the plans and used really well. When it comes to the arrangement of industrial plans and the allocation of materials, equipment and funds, priority must be given to guaranteeing that the needs of innovation and transformation are met.

10. War of Annihilation in Capital Construction

Resolute measures must be adopted to work out a set of strict management systems to settle this problem.

1. Both central departments and localities must arrange their capital construction investments and capital construction projects around the objectives of struggle for the next five and ten years. They must not depart from this general goal and go their own way. They must take into account the possibilities of the state with regard to material resources, finances and manpower, and not go beyond these possibilities. They must not do everything at the same time without an order of priorities. They must all implement the policy of building large, medium- and small-sized enterprises simultaneously and using modern and indigenous methods simultaneously. They must not go against this policy and instead pursue what is called big, modern and complete.

2. Starting in 1976, large and medium-sized projects to be undertaken each year are to be strictly limited to under XX [sic] projects. Projects to be completed and commissioned into production each year should be guaranteed to range from XX projects to XX projects. The average construction cycle is to be shortened from X years now to X

years. New projects must be strictly controlled, and projects under construction should be examined and cleared one by one, so that those projects which are not urgently needed or conditions do not measure up may be suspended or delayed.

3. All capital construction projects, including those financed with funds raised by the localities or departments themselves, must be incorporated into the state unified plans. Large and medium-sized projects should be approved by the state, and small projects by the provincial, municipal and autonomous regional authorities. No region, department or unit will be allowed to undertake capital construction projects unless authorized, nor will they be allowed to expand the scale of the project, raise the standard of construction or alter the progress of construction unless authorized. No one has the right to use for other projects materials, equipment and funds earmarked for key projects of the state.

4. Rectify the channeling of funds. No one is allowed to use for capital construction purposes funds set aside for major repair and overhaul, liquid capital for production, earnings retained by enterprises to cover basic depreciation, profits and tax revenues that the enterprises should deliver to the state, and bank loans. Nor will anyone be allowed to ask the enterprises, communes and brigades for contributions to undertake capital construction. Capital construction banks are to be instructed to keep unified control of all capital construction appropriations and carry out their supervisory work well; they must refuse to make appropriations for projects and expenditures in contravention of state stipulations.

5. All construction projects must strictly follow the capital construction procedures. Without designs and without properly arranging for equipment, these projects must not be included in yearly plans and construction must not start. For large and medium-sized projects, complete sets of equipment must be properly arranged and supplied in time in accordance with the progress of construction; this task must be handled by specialized agencies.

6. Rectify capital construction management. From geological prospecting, through design and construction to taking delivery, it is necessary to set up strict rules and regulations and systems of responsibility. Efforts must be made to raise the labor productivity of construction and installation teams, speed up the progress of construction, guarantee engineering quality, lower engineering costs, raise the yield of investment, and overcome serious wastage.

11. Adoption of Advanced Technology

It is by the adoption of the most advanced technologies that the industrially backward countries catch up with the industrially advanced countries in the world. We must also do the same. Every department and every industry must know the world's advanced level and map out plans and measures for catching up with and surpassing it.

We must make a big effort to develop a mass movement for technical innovation and scientific experimentation. We must respect the pioneering spirit of the masses and pay attention to summing up, elevating and popularizing the achievements of innovation and creation of the masses. We must develop the backbone roles of specialized research agencies and forces and enable them to cooperate closely with the masses in studying and solving major scientific and technological problems of a crucial nature. Scientific research units under the Chinese Academy of Sciences and the various ministries of the State Council, if they are undertaking national tasks, must follow the system under which they are led principally by the Chinese Academy of Sciences and the various ministries of the State Council. Where they have been turned over to the local authorities, they must be taken back. It is necessary to strengthen the scientific research and technological management of industrial and mining enterprises. Large and medium-sized enterprises must have their own research and experimental organs. Some enterprises must also establish intermediary testing plants and experimental workshops. Small enterprises within a single city or several enterprises in combination may set up needed research and experimental organs. Technicians of enterprises should be regarded as production personnel and must not be considered as cadres detached from production or as non-production personnel. Scientific research forces of institutions of higher education must be put to the fullest use, and the policy of "letting a hundred flowers bloom and a hundred schools of thought contend" must be implemented in order to make science and technology flourish.

We must persist in the policy of combining study with independent creation. We must study with an open mind all advanced and fine things of foreign countries, import advanced technologies from foreign countries in a planned and appropriate way and turn them into our own in order to accelerate the development of the national economy. We must uphold the policy of maintaining independence, keeping the initiative in our hands and achieving rejuvenation through self-reliance, and oppose the slavish comprador philosophy and the doctrine of trailing behind others. But we must not allow ourselves to be cocky nor adopt a closed-door attitude and refuse to learn from the good things of foreign countries. All industrial departments and scientific research units must avail themselves of the opportune moment created for us by the victory of Chairman Mao's revolutionary line in foreign affairs and master as fast as possible new technologies that we require urgently.

In regard to the importation of advanced technologies from foreign countries, we must train the necessary technical forces to master them as speedily as possible. In accordance with the principle of "first, use; second, criticize; third, convert; and fourth, create," we must, in the course of applying them, know them, transform them and develop them. We must oppose copying and applying them mechanically, and we must also oppose the practice of transforming them without first mastering them.

New technology, new inventions and new creations must be kept secret and there must be a system for this. But let there be no mutual blockade between departments and enterprises.

12. Increasing Export of Industrial and Mineral Products

If we are to import more advanced technologies from abroad, we must increase exports and raise the proportion of industrial and mineral products among export commodities.

Every industrial department must study the requirements of the international market and energetically increase the output of products which can be exported and have a high exchange value. We must develop production as fast as possible and increase our exports as much as possible. We must not consider only our import requirements without considering the need to increase export resources. Our country mainly emphasizes the domestic market and considers the external market to be supplementary. But the external market is very important and must not be neglected.

In order to accelerate the exploitation of our coal and petroleum, it is possible that on the condition of equality and mutual benefit and in accordance with accepted practices of international trade such as deferred payment and installment payment, we may sign long-term contracts with foreign countries and designate several production points, where they will supply complete sets of modern equipment required by us and then we will pay for them with the coal and oil we produce.

13. From Each According to His Ability, To Each According to His Work

On the question of wages, our Party's consistent policy has been to oppose not only wide differentials between high and low wages but also egalitarianism in respect to wages.

We must restrict bourgeois rights, oppose the extension of differences, and oppose material incentives. Failure to do this will aid the growth of capitalist elements as well as endanger the consolidation of the dictatorship of the proletariat.

We cannot restrict bourgeois rights by ignoring the material and spiritual conditions at the present stage, by rejecting the principles of to each according to his work, by disavowing the necessary differences and by practicing egalitarianism. Egalitarianism does not work now and will not work in the future.

From each according to his ability, to each according to his work, and he who does not work shall not eat--these are socialist principles. At the present stage, these principles basically meet the needs of the development of the productive forces and must be resolutely enforced. Equal pay for all without regard for the nature of one's work, one's ability and one's contribution will not be conducive to mobilization of the socialist initiative of the broad masses.

We must gradually raise the wages of the staff and workers receiving low wages and reduce the gap between high and low wages.

We must enforce the system of regular promotions. Every year or every two years we should raise the wages of a number of staff and workers in accordance with the attitude of the workers toward labor, their technical and vocational capabilities, and their contribution in labor and work, in accordance with the number of promotions granted in the state plan, and after evaluation by the masses and approval by the leadership.

We must give personal allowances to those who work under bad working conditions, such as working in high temperatures, atop tall structures, underground, in the wilderness, facing a danger of poisoning and other occupational hazards, and to those whose labor intensity is great.

We must gradually reform the existing wage system on the basis of investigations and study and summing up experiences.

All enterprises must persist in putting politics in command and urge the staff and workers to work hard for building a powerful socialist mother country and supporting world revolution, to establish a communist attitude toward labor, and to handle correctly the relationships between personal and collective interests and between immediate and long-range interests. We must not separate "to each according to his work" from "from each according to his ability." We must explain to the broad masses that we are still a developing country, that our living standard can only be improved on the basis of developing production and raising labor productivity, and that we must continue to display the fine tradition of hard work and plain living.

14. Concern for the Well-being of Staff and Workers

Leaders at various levels must attend to production and livelihood simultaneously. They must put the problems of the livelihood of the masses on their daily agenda for discussion. Where problems can be solved, they must mobilize the masses to solve them actively by themselves. It is utterly wrong to adopt an indifferent attitude toward the difficulties in the livelihood of the masses. The Party committee of every enterprise should have one principal responsible comrade to attend to matters relating to livelihood.

It is necessary, according to plan, to step up the building of staff and workers' dormitories and urban public utilities. Funds earmarked by the state for these purposes must not be used for other purposes. Local authorities should use more of the funds they have raised by themselves for these purposes.

We must actively improve the operation of social collective welfare undertakings such as mess halls, nurseries, and medical and health services. We must organize well spare-time educational and cultural, recreational and sports activities. We must make a success of birth control.

Efforts must be made to improve the supply of subsidiary foodstuffs in cities and in industrial and mining enterprises. Large and medium-sized cities must set up subsidiary foodstuff bases and gradually establish large-scale modern pig farms and chicken farms.

We must solve step by step the problem of husband and wife working in separate places for a long time.

When a worker retires or dies, one of his sons or daughters may be employed to fill his place provided that the conditions of employment are met.

We must make a success of labor protection, improve working conditions, and insure safety in production. Protection for women workers must be given attention.

We must resolutely eliminate the "three wastes," protect the environment, and protect the physical health of the staff and workers. Unless proper arrangements are made for the disposal of the "three wastes," permission will not be granted for construction of new projects. In old cities and existing enterprises, the problem of pollution must be solved according to plan.

Attention must be given to combining labor and rest.

15. Red and Expert

It is impossible to realize the great historical task of building our country into a modern and powerful socialist country without a large number of people who are high in political consciousness and proficient technically and vocationally.

Chairman Mao pointed out long ago: "As between politics and vocation, politics is predominant and primary. We must oppose the tendency to ignore politics, but it also won't do to know nothing about technique and business. Our comrades, whether they work in industry, agriculture, commerce or in culture and education, must learn some techniques and vocational skills, become old hands and make themselves both Red and expert." All cadres must respond to Chairman Mao's call and, through their own practical action, lead the masses of workers and scientific and technical personnel to take the road to being Red and expert.

The masses of workers must arm themselves with Marxism-Leninism-Mao Tsetung Thought and make an effort to study and master production techniques so that they will become laborers with high class consciousness, a strong sense of organization and discipline and technical proficiency and play their role as the main force in the three major revolutionary movements.

Scientists and technicians must persist in integrating themselves with the workers and peasants. They must make an effort to transform their world outlook and wholeheartedly serve the people. They must study science and technology and become well versed in their vocation. All those who are really willing to serve the socialist cause must be trusted and assisted in solving all kinds of problems that must be solved so that they will devote themselves to studying some things and actively develop their talent. All their achievements must be affirmed, and we must ardently help them overcome their shortcomings. In the case of those scientists and technicians who have improperly changed their occupation, an investigation must be carried out. It is utterly wrong for some units to pay no serious attention to scientists and technicians and to fail to bring their role into play.

Party committees at all levels must commend those advanced personalities who are both Red and expert. They must criticize and educate those people who ignore politics and fail to study techniques and vocational work. They must create a climate favorable to the study of Marxism-Leninism-Mao Tsetung Thought and to technical and vocational research. It is particularly necessary to pay attention to combining political and technical studies, and not to set one against the other. Conditions must be actively created for the masses of staff and workers to become both Red and expert.

16. Discipline

Discipline is a guarantee for the execution of the line. "Among the people, it won't do to be without freedom, nor without discipline; it won't do to be without democracy, nor without centralization. Such unity between democracy and centralization and between freedom and discipline is our system of democratic centralism."

Now, discipline has been lax in many respects. This produces a very bad effect and causes great harm. We must strengthen the sense of discipline and struggle against all violations of policies, regulations, unified plans, financial discipline and labor discipline.

The masses of staff and workers must abide by discipline consciously.

All Party members, Communist Youth League members and particularly leading cadres at various levels ought to set an example in observing discipline.

We must support and commend those comrades who seriously carry out policies and regulations and who dare to uphold principles, and strictly prohibit attacks on or reprisals against them.

Those who violate discipline must be solemnly criticized and educated. Those whose offense is serious must be punished. We must sanction those who violate the law and discipline in accordance with Party rules and state laws and not be lenient.

17. Methods of Work and Style of Work

"Go deeper a little, gain experience and promote the whole situation"--this is a Marxist-Leninist method of work that our Party has long applied effectively. We must also adopt this method in industry.

There are good typical examples, good experiences, and a large number of new socialist things in various localities and departments. Leaders at various levels must go deep among the masses and devotedly seek out the advanced experiences among the masses, sum them up and popularize them so as to encourage the masses to march forward and raise production continuously to new levels. In many localities and departments where this has been done, work has been carried out with vigor and good results. But there are still quite a number of units that are not good in doing so. There, the cadres are accustomed to sitting in offices and issuing orders; they do not comprehend either the overall situation or typical examples. They must change their methods of work and style of work.

While grasping the advanced, we must give attention to the work of transforming backward units.

In accordance with Chairman Mao's directive that "under the guidance of the general line, it is necessary to work out a whole set of specific principles, policies and measures" and by means of "from the masses and to the masses," we must formulate industrial management rules, enterprise management regulations and work regulations for all industries and trades.

We must be practical, guard against empty talk, reduce the number of conferences, hold short conferences, and make short speeches. We must not hold discussions without reaching decisions and putting them into effect. Our work must be penetrating, meticulous, and practical. We must oppose working in a shallow and not deep manner, roughly and not carefully, ostentatiously and not realistically. We must promote the Tach'ing Oilfield's "three-honest, four-strict" style of work. We must dare to accept responsibility and oppose passing the buck around and doing things perfunctorily. We must be concerned about practical results and efficiency and oppose procrastination. We must have drive and stamina. We must not tell lies.

18. The Way of Thinking

We must promote materialist dialectics and oppose metaphysics. We must make an effort to avoid one-sidedness and partialities. We must look at a problem from many sides, not from one side alone. We must see the essence through the appearance. We must be alert against one tendency covering up another tendency.

We must adopt an analytical attitude toward all things, protect correct things and criticize wrong ones. We must neither affirm nor negate everything indiscriminately, without finding out the truth.

We must seek truth from facts, step up investigations and study, make thinking compatible with objective reality, and continue to know and master the objective laws of socialist construction.

We must pay serious attention to both positive and negative experiences. By comparing successes with failures, we shall completely or relatively completely recognize those things we now either do not recognize or recognize incompletely.

OUTLINE SUMMARY REPORT OF THE WORK OF THE ACADEMY OF SCIENCES*

The entire system of the Chinese Academy of Sciences now comprises 93 scientific research institutes and a total of thirty-six thousand staff members, of whom twenty-five thousand are scientific and technical personnel. Since merging with the State Scientific Commission in 1970, the Academy has also become responsible for reconstituting (kuei-k'ou) and administering scientific and technical work across the country. We are now reporting back on the orientation and tasks of scientific research work in the Academy, the problem of how to implement thoroughly Chairman Mao's revolutionary line on scientific and technical research, and the problem of readjustment necessary in order to implement [this line]. We will report back separately on the planning of scientific and technical work in the whole country and also on the problem of reconstituting (kuei-k'ou) and administering [scientific work].

I. The Orientation and Tasks of Research Work in the Chinese Academy of Sciences

With the kind attention of Chairman Mao and the Party Center and guided by Chairman Mao's revolutionary line, the socialist Chinese Academy of Sciences has, in the past twenty-six years, grown from nothing and developed from a small to a large force, [now] forming a fair-sized contingent with a definite level of political consciousness and vocational skill. We have conducted work in a series of major scientific and technical areas and scored great achievements; we have accumulated rich experience in advancing the cause of socialist science and have made relatively rapid progress. However, the interference and sabotage of the counter-revolutionary revisionist lines of Liu Shao-ch'i and Lin Piao have seriously affected our orientation and speed of development. During the Great Proletarian Cultural Revolution and the movement to criticize Lin Piao and Confucius, we criticized and liquidated

---

* "K'o-hsüeh yüan kung-tso hui-pao t'i-kang." Source: Ming-pao News Daily, Hong Kong, serialized in seven installments from July 5-11, 1977. Translated by Ai Ping, with emendations by Kenneth Lieberthal. This translation appears in Chinese Law and Government (forthcoming in 1978), and is used with the permission of M. E. Sharpe, Publishers. This is the draft of the "Outline Summary Report" completed by Hu Ch'iao-mu by early September 1975.

their counter-revolutionary revisionist lines and cleared the way for the correct and rapid development of work in our Academy.

At present our Academy faces a new situation and has before it new tasks. The great leader Chairman Mao and the Party Center are calling upon us to accomplish the comprehensive modernization of agriculture, industry, national defense and science and technology before the end of the century so that our national economy will advance in the front ranks of the world and our country will be built into a modernized, powerful socialist state. Both the international and domestic situations require us to race against time and accelerate our speed so as to make the national economy catch up. No matter whether talking about the present or the longer term, both the national economy and defense construction are posing a large number of scientific and technical problems. These require the scientific research front to organize its forces rapidly so as to solve these problems in a well-planned way and in good time. It is also necessary to use scientific and technical modernization to accelerate modernization of the national economy and defense construction. There is no denying that, compared both with the requirements of socialist construction and with the advanced levels in the world, the current strength and level of scientific research in our country lag considerably behind. We have not yet been able to extricate ourselves from a state of passivity regarding a series of major and crucial problems of science and technology. If [we] cannot quicken our speed and push on with scientific research work so as to hasten the process of catching up with and surpassing [advanced world levels], the speed of both national economic development and defense construction as a whole will be affected.

In light of the foregoing demands, we think the basic tasks in the ten years ahead for the Chinese Academy of Sciences, which functions as the comprehensive natural science research center in our country, can be generalized into the following three major facets: in coordination with departments concerned, actively undertake certain major and comprehensive scientific research tasks required by the national economy and defense construction; open up a number of newly emerging areas of science and technology and make great efforts to score certain achievements of major use; develop basic science so as to lay a solid theoretical foundation for work in the above two facets and determine the direction for further progress. Based on the tasks stated above, we must immediately start drawing up a ten-year plan for scientific research in our Academy. Now, we are presenting some preliminary and incomplete ideas in this regard:

1. Actively Undertake Certain Major and Comprehensive Scientific Research Tasks Required by the National Economy and Defense Construction: The Chinese Academy of Sciences has the advantage of being able to coordinate several branches of learning to undertake one common research project and also has access to certain new techniques. We should make full use of these favorable conditions to conduct extensive cooperation with the outside departments concerned. By taking immediate needs as our major concern while also considering long-term objectives, we should strive together [with these departments] actively to do research on the solutions for certain important problems of science and technology relating to industry, agriculture, medicine and public health, and defense construction. For example, in the industrial sphere we should conduct research on the laws governing the formation of minerals, new methods for mineral prospecting and the problem of comprehensive utilization of some mineral resources; do research on the development of certain metal materials, materials of high polymer synthetic compounds and silicate materials; and also do research on such scientific problems as developing [the techniques of] automation and remote control in industrial production and among the communications and transport departments. In the agricultural realm, we must utilize new achievements in modern biology and other branches of learning [to facilitate] progress in mechanizing agriculture, breeding new varieties, improving soil and water conservation, opening up new manure sources, developing new types of feeds, preventing and controlling plant disease and insect damage, and forecasting disastrous weather; these will provide new ways to increase agricultural production. In the area of medicine and public health, we should conduct research on the causes of tumors, the theory of acupuncture anaesthesia, and family planning, and we should develop new types of medicine. As for defense construction, we must coordinate our efforts with the defense departments to do research on and manufacture certain new materials, elements (yuan-chien) and equipment needed by the most advanced branches of defense technology; we should also explore new technical approaches, and so forth.

2. Open Up a Number of Newly Emerging Areas of Science and Technology: In the Twelve-Year Science Plan for 1956-1967, the Chinese Academy of Sciences took some urgent measures to advance the work in the fields of semi-conductors, computers, automation, and electronics; later, the Academy also grappled with technical work related to lasers and infrared light. All this played a leading role in promoting newly emerging branches of science and technology in our

country and facilitated the development of corresponding new branches of industry. In the next ten years, we should again select a group of newly emerging areas of science and technology that will play a major role in enabling our national economy and national defense to catch up with and surpass [advanced world levels]; we can coordinate with the relevant departments, concentrate our strength, and make major breakthroughs. These include such areas as the technology of scientific observation in space (including satellites for astronomy, earth resource satellites, meteorological satellites, and the corresponding techniques of distance induction, etc.), information theory and cybernetics (including research on and the manufacture of a giant computer capable of performing a hundred million calculations per second), technology related to new sources of energy, environmental science, cloning (fang-sheng hsüeh), and so forth.

3. Devote All Our Efforts to Developing Research in the Basic Sciences: As a comprehensive base for basic science research, the Chinese Academy of Sciences should, on the basis of broad and in-depth practice, develop scientific theories, and moreover should use these as a guide to practice. Scientific research institutions of the state and of various industrial departments demand that our Academy shoulder even more tasks in this regard so as to help solve many of the key issues that have been encountered in the advancement of the various branches of applied science. We should conduct in-depth key point exploration on the cutting edge of such fields as mathematics, astronomy, mechanics, physics, chemistry, biology, oceanography, and earth sciences, as well as on the series of sciences peripheral to these fields. We should also strive to make appropriate contributions to certain major problems in present-day scientific theory. These include elemental particles, quantum-chemistry, cosmogony, the origin of the cell, the essence of physiological and mental activities, the theory of heredity, cybernetics, and so forth.

The tasks we face are both glorious and formidable. We must actively mobilize and organize the broad masses of the entire Academy to pluck up their revolutionary spirit, unite in battle, race against time, strive for speed, and energetically struggle to fulfill the historic task of catching up with and surpassing the advanced world levels of science and technology.

II. Resolutely and Comprehensively Implement Chairman Mao's Revolutionary Line on Science and Technology

The key to whether or not the Chinese Academy of Sciences can mobilize all its forces to complete quickly and effectively the above-mentioned fighting tasks lies in whether or not we can resolutely and comprehensively implement Chairman Mao's proletarian revolutionary line as well as his revolutionary line in science and technology. Chairman Mao has formulated for our Party a proletarian revolutionary line, a line which the various departments in the entire Party, including the Party organization in the Academy, must resolutely, comprehensively, and thoroughly implement. At the same time, Chairman Mao has also issued a series of important directives regarding how to achieve greater, faster, better and more economical results in the development of scientific and technological work in our country. He put forward a comprehensive, Marxist-Leninist revolutionary line in science and technology, the main points of which are:

1. It expounds the important role that scientific and technological work plays in thoroughly implementing the Party's basic line, in combating and preventing revisionism and in consolidating the proletarian dictatorship. "Class struggle, the struggle for production, and scientific experiment are the three great revolutionary movements for building a mighty socialist country. These movements are a sure guarantee that Communists will be free from bureaucratism and immune to revisionism and dogmatism, and [that they] will forever remain invincible. They are reliable guarantees that the proletariat will be able to unite with the broad working masses and implement a democratic dictatorship."

2. It sets the great goal for us that our country's science and technology "must catch up with and surpass advanced world levels in the not-so-distant future." "We cannot just take the beaten track traversed by other countries in the development of technology and trail behind them at a snail's pace. We must break away from convention and adopt as many advanced techniques as possible." "Science and technology are productive forces." "We must fight the battle of science and technology, and must fight it well. If we do not handle our science and technology, the productive forces cannot be raised."

3. "To attain this great goal, [we] need to have an adequate number of outstanding scientific and technological experts." "In order to achieve

socialism, the working class must have its own contingent of technical cadres, must have its own contingent of professors, teachers, scientists, news reporters, writers, artists, and Marxist theoreticians. This is a great contingent, and insufficient manpower will not do."

4. In developing scientific and technological work it is necessary to carry out "integrating intellectuals with the masses of workers and peasants" and realize the "three-in-one combination" of leading cadres, the masses of workers and peasants, and science and technical personnel. "The lowly are most intelligent and the elite are most ignorant." We should encourage the workers, peasants, new and old cadres, and intellectuals of the entire country to "wipe out their sense of inferiority, get rid of the mentality of belittling themselves, and break down blind faith, so as to cultivate an invincible creative spirit of daring to think, daring to speak, and daring to act."

5. We "must put proletarian politics in command," persist in "unifying politics with technology," and adhere to [the requirement of] "both red and expert." We "must be opposed to armchair politicians on the one hand and reject practitioners who lose their bearings on the other." "Ideological work and political work are the guarantees for the fulfillment of economic work and technical work; they are for the purpose of serving the economic base. Furthermore, ideology and politics are the commander, the soul [of everything]. Once we relax a bit in our ideological and political work, economic work and technical work are bound to go astray."

6. We must adhere to the Marxist line concerning cognition and achieve "unity of theory and practice." Marxist philosophy "emphasizes the dependence of theory on practice, emphasizes that practice is the basis of theory, and that theory in turn serves practice." "To fully reflect a thing in its totality, to reflect its essence, to reflect its inherent laws, it is necessary through the exercise of thought to reconstruct the rich data of sense perception, discarding the dross and selecting the essential, eliminating the false and retaining the true, proceeding from the one to the other and from the outside to the inside, in order to form a system of concepts and theories--it is necessary to make a leap from perceptual to rational knowledge." We "must strengthen theoretical research and have special people do this work. It will not do if we do not engage in theoretical [studies]." At the same time, we must correctly handle the relationship between popularization and elevation and implement, "raising

standards based on popularization," and "popularization guided by raising standards."

7. We must carry out scientific and technical work by maintaining independence and keeping the initiative in our own hands and via [a policy of] self-reliance; "Down with the slave mentality! Bury dogmatism!" "We must absorb all the good experiences and good science and technology of foreign countries and put them to our own use. It is wrong to refuse to learn from foreign countries; of course, it is also wrong to place blind faith in foreign countries and regard everything foreign as good."

8. We must implement [the policy of] letting a hundred flowers bloom and a hundred schools of thought contend. Different forms and styles of art are free to develop and different schools of science can freely contend. Questions of right and wrong in arts and science can be solved through free discussion and through practice in artistic and scientific circles and should not be resolved via adopting simple methods. The principle of letting a hundred flowers bloom and a hundred schools of thought contend cannot weaken the dominant position of Marxism in the field of ideology; rather, it will strengthen its position.

9. "In order to meet fully the needs of the new society and to unite as one with workers and peasants, the intellectuals must continue to remold themselves so as gradually to abandon their bourgeois world outlook and embrace the proletarian communist world outlook. The change of one's world outlook is a fundamental change." "You who study natural science should master the use of dialectics."

10. "Among the Party, the government, the army, the people and the students and in the east, west, south and north, and center, it is the Party that leads everything." "The whole Party should resolutely struggle to study scientific knowledge and unite as one with non-Party intellectuals so as to catch up quickly with the advanced world levels of science." "Only if we can understand more about Marxism, understand more about natural science, in a word, understand more about the laws governing the objective world and thus commit fewer mistakes of subjectivism will our work of revolution and construction definitely attain its goal."

Chairman Man's proletarian revolutionary line, including as one of its component parts the revolutionary line in science and technology, is a beacon guiding our scientific and technological work in its advance along the correct direction. By thoroughly implementing unswervingly and without vacillating, comprehensively and not one-sidedly, the line and policies laid down by Chairman Mao, we can surely push forward scientific and technological work relatively quickly, can surely establish at a relatively rapid pace a scientific and technological contingent that is both red and expert, and can surely make relatively great contributions to socialist revolution and socialist construction.

It is necessary energetically to carry out systematic and accurate propaganda on Chairman Mao's revolutionary line in science and technology, and to pay attention to preventing and overcoming any deviation from, mutilation of, or distortion of this line. For instance, we must criticize any tendency to pay no attention to politics. It is incorrect not to wage struggle against this tendency. On the other hand, it is also incorrect if we neither require nor encourage scientific and technical personnel to study science and technology and conduct research [in this field] for the sake of the revolution. We must criticize the tendency to belittle [the role of] the masses in scientific research work. It is incorrect if we do not energetically overcome this and conscientiously urge scientific and technical personnel to integrate themselves with the masses of workers and peasants and to learn from them. On the other hand, it is also incorrect if we do not bring into play the role of specialized scientific research organizations and of specialists. We must criticize the tendency of scientific research work to separate itself from reality. It is incorrect if we do not resolutely rectify this tendency and fail actively to guide the scientific and technical personnel to do research on and resolve the urgent needs of actual production. On the other hand, it is also incorrect if we ignore or deny the importance of research on basic theory and the necessity of laboratory work.

We must persist in reforming the world outlook of the intellectuals. It is incorrect to hold that intellectuals have just about adequately remolded themselves. On the other hand, it is also incorrect to keep away from using the intellectuals while talking about reforming them, contending that the intellectuals can only be used after they have been remolded. We must stress the guiding role of Marxist philosophy in relation to natural science and advocate that scientific research personnel study the dialectics of nature. It is incorrect to regard philosophy as not being of guiding significance for natural science research. On the other hand, it is also incorrect to believe that concrete conclusions to specific scientific problems can be arrived at by simple inference and computation in accordance with some general principles of philosophy and without having to conduct a great deal of hard work so as to establish precise evidence and arguments [grounded] in science itself, etc.

Because the Academy of Sciences is a place where intellectuals mass together, the bourgeois intellectuals there are relatively great in number, and both bourgeois thought and the idea of the bourgeois right have exerted a relatively deep influence. Both at present and for a long time to come, the tendencies to be divorced from proletarian politics, from the masses of workers and peasants, and from the reality of production as well as the tendency to expand the three major differences may exist, and, if we relax just a bit, may rise to the surface. Revisionism still poses the major danger to our Academy. We must fully recognize this and constantly be vigilant so that we will never repeat the mistakes of the past. Nonetheless, it is only by adhering to the standpoint of firmly and comprehensively carrying out Chairman Mao's revolutionary line in science and technology that we can correctly and effectively carry on the struggle against the above-mentioned tendency toward revisionism. Any over-simplified and crude attitudes and methods, any bragging, any substitution of personal feelings for policy, or any willful, one-sided interpretation of Chairman Mao's revolutionary line in science and technology will inevitably create ideological confusion and cause damage to our work. These might even lead to a serious weakening or obliteration of scientific and technological work, which would virtually be separating [this work] from the political needs of the proletariat, from the needs of socialist construction, and from the needs of the masses of the people. This could still sink down into revisionism again.

The Party organization in the Chinese Academy of Sciences should lead and educate the masses to systematically, penetratingly and repeatedly study and acquire a true grasp of the series of Chairman Mao's important instructions regarding science and technology. At the same time, this should be combined with the study and understanding of relevant, important arguments [made] by Marx, Engels and Lenin. We ought to wage long-term, persistent struggles against various revisionist manifestations and influences. We must strive to master utilizing materialist dialectics implementing the Party's line and policies and handling the various "unity of opposites" relationships. We must oppose metaphysics, make concrete analysis of concrete situations, take notice [of the fact] that one tendency covers up another tendency, and prevent going from one extreme to the other. All this will facilitate leading the vast numbers of cadres and masses to raise their understanding and unify their thinking so as to implement Chairman Mao's proletarian revolutionary line as well as his revolutionary line in science and technology resolutely, comprehensively, and thoroughly.

III. Regarding the Problem of Rectifying (cheng-tun) the Academy of Sciences

The Academy of Sciences must carry out rectification ideologically, politically and organizationally in order to fulfill the formidable tasks that the Party and state have entrusted to us and also to implement Chairman Mao's proletarian revolutionary line and his revolutionary line in science and technology, resolutely, comprehensively, and thoroughly. The Great Proletarian Cultural Revolution has won a great victory in our Academy. The broad masses, cadres, and scientific and technical personnel have greatly enhanced their consciousness of class struggle and line struggle and urgently demand to [be able to] make more contributions to socialism. Many of them have already done some beneficial work in the scientific and technical research dimensions of a portion of economic and defense construction and similarly with a portion of theoretical research. The general situation is good. However, the task of struggle-criticism-transformation must be continually deepened, and rectification means deepening struggle-criticism-transformation. Based on the seven "yes or no" comparative check-ups set forth in Document 13 [i.e., chung-fa #13] issued by the Center, the Academy of Sciences still has the following relatively serious problems: There are quite a few mistaken ideas about Chairman Mao's proletarian revolutionary line, even to the point where distortions and counteracting [ideas] exist; the Party's policies regarding intellectuals and cadres still have not been implemented correctly and thoroughly; to varying degrees the phenomena of softness, laziness, and laxity exist in the leading groups at different levels; bourgeois factionalism is still very serious in certain departments and units; the militant role of Party organizations has suffered damage, discipline is lax, and unity has eroded. Unless this situation is changed, the task of consolidating the dictatorship of the proletariat cannot be fulfilled and scientific research work cannot be performed properly. We must rely on the broad masses of the entire Academy and resolutely rectify well the Academy of Sciences. This is what the Party earnestly expects of the Academy and is also the urgent demand of the broad masses in the Academy.

In substance, rectification has the following five aspects:

1. Link up with reality, study conscientiously, expose contradictions, and unfold criticism and self-criticism.

   Immediately organize the broad masses, link up closely with reality and, focusing on the difficult problems in which our Academy is now embroiled, penetratingly study Chairman Mao's three important directives regarding theoretical problems, stability and unity, and pushing the national economy forward; penetratingly study the series of Chairman Mao's instructions regarding scientific and technological work; and penetratingly study the series of documents recently issued by the Center. In the course of study, seriously and conscientiously unfold criticism and self-criticism, face problems squarely and expose contradictions; firmly grasp problems related to the Party's line, guidelines and policies, and also grasp firmly questions concerning the Party's organizational principles; hold fast to the main orientation of the struggle and guard against any interference and resistance [stemming] from bourgeois factionalism. In the course of study and conducting criticism and self-criticism, leading cadres at various levels and all Party members must set themselves as examples and courageously move at the head of the masses. They must oppose mistaken attitudes such as trying to muddle through, adopting a wait and see policy, or acting in a worldly wise manner so as to play safe. We must, via study and debates between different views, uphold the truth, correct mistakes, raise our consciousness, achieve unanimity in our thinking, and resolutely unite on the basis of Chairman Mao's revolutionary line.

2. Conscientiously fulfill the Party's policies regarding intellectuals and cadres.

   Within a short period, adopt effective measures so as to conscientiously fulfill within the entire sphere of the Academy the Party's policy of uniting with, educating and remolding the intellectuals. On the basis of penetrating study, the various units must unify their thinking, conduct a comprehensive survey of how things stand regarding implementation of the Party's policy on intellectuals in their respective units, and make appropriate decisions so as to bring into full play the socialist activism of the broad masses of intellectuals. [We] must create necessary conditions to enable them to conduct scientific activities and raise their scientific level, must guarantee them necessary time and also show concern for their livelihood. Simultaneous with utilizing them, it is necessary to continue to grasp [their] ideological remolding and persist in the orientation of integrating intellectuals with workers and peasants.

Keep a firm grasp on fulfilling the Party's cadre policy. Assignments and readjustments must earnestly be made for all those who can work but either have not been assigned jobs or have been assigned to inappropriate jobs. At the same time, we must educate the cadres to abide by their assignments and be willing to work at either higher or lower levels. Strive to settle as soon as possible the cases concerning persons for whom no conclusion was reached during the movement to purify class ranks and the movement to criticize Lin Piao and those persons whose cases need to be re-checked. When making a decision on a case or re-checking, it is necessary strictly to distinguish between and correctly handle the two qualitatively different types of contradictions and to do a really good job of the various aspects of ideological work.

3. Strengthen the proletarian Party spirit and criticize and eliminate bourgeois factionalism.

At present the Party organization in our Academy urgently needs rectification. Of the demands of rectification, the major one is to raise every Party member's consciousness of continuing the revolution so that the Party members can really become fighters of "a vigorous vanguard organization that is able to lead the proletariat and the revolutionary masses in their struggle against the class enemy." [We must] demand that Party members persist in [maintaining] the proletariat's revolutionary integrity, and dare to lead the masses in waging resolute struggles against all bourgeois ideas and work styles as well as against all kinds of evil winds and noxious trends. It is necessary to observe strictly the Party's political discipline and organizational discipline and resolutely correct such evil phenomena as refusing to execute, support or propagate the Party's line and policies, even to the extent of damaging the interests of the Party, the state and the masses; [we must also] resolutely correct the evil phenomena of violating the Party's democratic centralism by the minority not obeying the majority, individuals not obeying the organization, the lower levels not obeying higher levels, and Party organizations not obeying the Central Committee. Every [Party] branch must become a strong fighting bastion that resolutely executes the Party's line and decisions. Admission of new members to the Party must be made in strict conformity with stipulations laid down in the Party's constitution, and we must not allow people who do not meet the conditions of Party membership to join the Party.

Bourgeois factionalism is absolutely incompatible with the proletarian Party spirit. It is exactly what the broad masses extremely detest and strongly object to. To engage in bourgeois factionalism is precisely to practice revisionism, to restore capitalism, to split the Party, and to do something which is neither above-board nor straightforward. On no account should a Communist practice peaceful coexistence with bourgeois factionalism. Despite whatever denials they make, those who are seriously affected by bourgeois factionalism actually know only about their faction and nothing about the Party. They gather their trusted supporters around themselves, sit on mountain tops, hand out official posts, make lavish promises, and push aside those who disagree with them. They contend for fame, gain, power and position even to the extent of distorting the Party's line and resisting the Party's leadership. We must by our forthright actions uphold (and not simply verbally recognize) the three basic principles: "Practice Marxism, and not revisionism; unite, and don't split; be open and above-board, and do not intrigue and conspire." [We should] talk about the [Party's] line, the whole situation, Party spirit, unity, and discipline, and wage resolute and serious struggles against the various manifestations of bourgeois factionalism. We must implement the consistent policies taught by Chairman Mao towards comrades engaged in bourgeois factionalism: "Unity-criticism-unity," and "Learn from past mistakes to avoid future ones, and cure the sickness to save the patient." So long as they can take a correct attitude towards the exposure and criticism from the masses, earnestly recognize and correct their mistakes and make a thorough and clean break with bourgeois factionalism, we must warmly unite with them and work together with them. We must not in an unprincipled way accommodate those individuals who persist in their errors and continually engage in severe factional activities even while the rectification is underway. Those who refuse to reform after repeated education must resolutely be transferred [to other posts].

Rectify and perfect the leading groups.

Strictly following Chairman Mao's five requirements for revolutionary successors and observing the principles of "from all corners of the country" and of combining the old, the middle-aged and the young, we will select and promote to leading posts at various levels those comrades who are strong in Party spirit and can put daring above all else, who are able to uphold the Party's line and policies and arduously study Marxism-Leninism and Mao Tse-tung Thought, and who diligently pursue vocational skill, actively work, and maintain close ties with the masses. We must also pay attention to cultivating, selecting and promoting cadres who are relatively young but are good in politics, are vocationally knowledgeable, and have drive and organizational skill; these should participate in the leadership of scientific research work in the various institutes and offices.

5. Structural rectification.

The Academy of Sciences must first direct its primary effort to running its subordinate research institutions well, while at the same time also doing a good job of bringing together and administering scientific research work across the country. Based on the work tasks mentioned above, the Academy, departments, and organs must be rectified to change the currently-existing phenomena of overstaffed and overlapping organizations so that we can strive to "attain the five objectives of simplification, unity, efficiency, frugality, and opposition to bureaucratism."

A portion of the research organizations of the Academy of Sciences that have been transferred to local [management] are key point research institutes that mainly undertake national-level tasks. In order to facilitate a concentration of work force and over-all planning and proper arrangement, we propose to place these under the dual leadership of the Academy and the locality, with the Academy's leadership being primary.

The Science and Technology University has been transferred to Anhui Province and is now under the dual leadership of the provincial Party committee and the Academy. In order to train, in a planned way, vocational cadres urgently needed in scientific research work, we propose that the Academy exercise primary leadership over this university.

For many years quite a number of specialized units in our Academy have not recruited any new forces. The average age of staff and workers is already close to forty and that of the research personnel is even somewhat older. We urgently need to adopt a series of effective measures to solve this serious problem.

We firmly believe that, under the leadership of Chairman Mao and the Party Center and relying on the broad masses, we can certainly do a good job of rectifying the Academy of Sciences. This will facilitate rapidly changing the Academy's face and will be beneficial for resolutely, comprehensively, and thoroughly implementing Chairman Mao's proletarian revolutionary line and his revolutionary line in science and technology; [it will also help us to be able] to shoulder the glorious and formidable tasks the Party and the state have entrusted to us.

The End

APPENDIX II

Known Central Documents, 1966-1977

I. Abbreviations for Central Documents Cosignatories*

A-PLA CRG	All-PLA Cultural Revolution Group
CCRG	Central Cultural Revolution Group
CMC	Central Military Commission
GFCCR	Group of Five in Charge of the Cultural Revolution
GPD	General Political Department
MAC	Military Affairs Committee
SC	State Council

*The CCP Central Committee is a signatory to each of these documents.

II. Sources

A. Format for citations: a: b (c)

a = source

b = page numbers, year, issue number

c = form:

CT	Chinese text
ET	English text
PCT	partial Chinese text
PET	partial English text
M	mentioned
*	title differs from that given in other sources cited for this text

B. Numbered abbreviations for sources

1. Documents of the Chinese Communist Party Central Committee, September 1956–April 1969, vol. 1. Hong Kong: Union Research Institute, 1971.

2. Chinese Communist Party Documents of the Great Proletarian Cultural Revolution, 1966-1967. Hong Kong: Union Research Institute, 1968.

3. Kung-fei wen-hua ta ko-ming chung-yao wen-chien hui-pien. Kuo-fang pu ch'ing-pao chü, 1968.

4. Kung-fei wen-hua ta ko-ming chung-yao wen-chien hsü-pien. Kuo-fang pu ch'ing-pao chü, 1969.

5. Michael Y. M. Kau, ed. The Lin Piao Affair: Power Politics and Military Coup. White Plains, N.Y.: International Arts and Sciences Press, Inc., 1975.

6. Ting Wang. Chung-kung wen-hua ta ko-ming tzu-liao hui-pien. Ming-pao, 1967-1972.

7. Chung-kung yen-chiu (formerly Fei-ch'ing yen-chiu). Taipei, Taiwan.

8. Chung-kung nien-pao (formerly Fei-ch'ing nien-pao). Taipei, Taiwan.

9. New China News Agency (NCNA).

10. Hung-ch'i. Peking.

11. Chinese Law and Government. White Plains, N.Y.: International Arts and Sciences Press.

12. Issues and Studies. Taipei, Taiwan.

13. Jen-min jih-pao. Peking.

14. FBIS/PRC.

15. Kuang-ming jih-pao. Peking.

16. Peking Review. Peking.

17. Peking Domestic Service.

18. *Chinese Record*.

19. *Ming-pao*. Hong Kong, unless otherwise indicated.

20. *Chung-yang jih-pao*. Taiwan.

21. Shanghai City Service.

22. Kunming Yunnan Provincial Service.

23. AFP. Hong Kong.

24. Chengchou Honan Provincial Service.

25. *Chung-kung chung-yang kuan-yü wu ch'an chieh-chi wen-hua ta ko-ming wen-chien hsüan-pien*. Yunnan sheng: Chiao-yü t'ing, 1967.

26. *New York Times*.

III. List of Known Central Documents, 1966-1967

Date of Issue	CD Number	Title	Cosignatories	Source
12 February 1966		Outline Report Concerning the Current Academic Discussion of the Group of Five in Charge of the Cultural Revolution		2: 3-6 (CT) 7-12 (ET)
16 May 1966		Circular of the Central Committee of the Chinese Communist Party		2: 13-19 (CT) 20-28 (ET)
16 May 1966		Comment of the CCP Central Committee on the Transmission of the Report of the Work Group of the Central Committee Concerning the Problem of Lo Jui-ch'ing's Mistakes		2: 29-30 (CT) 31-32 (ET)
3 June 1966		Decision of the CCP Central Committee on Reorganization of Peking Municipal Committee		6: 001 A (PCT)
13 June 1966		Circular of the CCP Central Committee and the State Council Concerning Reform in the Entrance Examination System of Higher Middle Schools	SC	6: 001 A (CT)

8 August 1966	Decision of the Central Committee of the CCP Concerning the Great Proletarian Cultural Revolution		2: 33-41 (CT) 42-54 (ET)
12 August 1966	Communique of the Eleventh Plenary Session of the Eighth Central Committee of the CCP		2: 55-61 (CT) 62-70 (ET)
5 September 1966	Circular on Teachers and Students of Various Locales before They Come to Peking for Visiting and Study	SC	3: 133-134 (CT)
8 September 1966	Regulations of the CCP Central Committee and the State Council Concerning the Protection of the Security of Party and State Secrets during the Great Cultural Revolution Movement	SC	2: 71 (CT) 72 (ET)
11 September 1966	Four-Point Decision Transmitted by the CCP Central Committee Appendix: Chairman Mao's "September 7" Directive		2: 73-74 (CT) 75-76 (ET)

Date of Issue	CD Number	Title	Cosignatories	Source
14 September 1966		Regulations of the CCP Central Committee Concerning the Great Cultural Revolution in the Countryside below the County Level		2: 77-78 (CT) 79-80 (ET)
18 September 1966		Circular of the CCP Central Committee on the Question of Wages for the Objects of Criticism and Struggle		2: 81 (CT) 82 (ET)
22 September 1966		Directive of the CCP Central Committee Concerning the Serious Study, Discussion, Comprehension and Application of Comrade Lin Piao's Speech by the Whole Party and the Whole Army		2: 83-84 (CT) 85-86 (ET)
5 October 1966		Urgent Directive of the Military Commission and the General Political Department Concerning the Great Proletarian Cultural Revolution in the Military Academies and Schools Appendix: Comment of the CCP Central Committee	CMC, GPD	2: 87-88 (CT) 89-92 (ET)
5 October 1966		Urgent Circular of the CCP Cen-	SC	3: 82-83 (CT)

	Council Concerning the Protection of Railway Transportation		
7 November 1966	Comment of the CCP Central Committee and the Central Cultural Revolution Group on the Transmission of "Comrade Ch'en Yung-kuei's Views on the Great Cultural Revolution in the Countryside"	CCRG	4: 64-68 (CT)
16 November 1966	Supplementary Regulations of the CCP Central Committee Concerning the Question of Handling Archive Material in the Great Proletarian Cultural Revolution		2: 101-102 (CT) 103-105 (ET) 3: 20-21 (CT)
16 November 1966	Circular of the CCP Central Committee and the State Council Concerning the Question of Revolutionary Teachers and Students Exchanging Revolutionary Experience	SC	2: 107-108 (CT) 109-111 (ET)
20 November 1966	Circular of the CCP Central Committee Concerning the Transmission of Important Notice of the CCP Peking Municipal Committee of November 18 Appendix: Important Notice		2: 121 (CT) 122-123 (ET)

Date of Issue	CD Number	Title	Cosignatories	Source
1 December 1966		Supplementary Circular of the CCP Central Committee and the State Council Concerning the Question of Exchange of Revolutionary Experience by Revolutionary Teachers and Students	SC	2: 125-126 (CT) 127-129 (ET)
9 December 1966		Ten Regulations of the CCP Central Committee Concerning Grasping Revolution and Promoting Production (Draft)		2: 131-132 (CT) 133-135 (ET)
15 December 1966		Directive of the CCP Central Committee Concerning the Great Proletarian Cultural Revolution in the Countryside (Draft)		2: 137-138 (CT) 139-142 (ET) 3: 83-85 (CT)
25 December 1966		Circular of the General Office of the CCP Central Committee		2: 143 (CT) 144 (ET) 3: 117 (CT)*
28 December 1966		Circular of the CCP Central Committee and the State Council Concerning the Prohibition of the Extensive Promotion of	SC	2: 145 (CT) 146 (ET)

31 December 1966		Circular of the CCP Central Committee and the State Council Concerning the Short-term Military and Political Training for Revolutionary Teachers and Students of Universities and Middle Schools	SC	2: 147-149 (CT) 150-153 (ET) 3: 115-117 (CT)
11 January 1967		Message of Greetings to Revolutionary Rebel Organizations in Shanghai	SC, CMC CCRG	2: 155-156 (CT) 157-158 (ET)
11 January 1967	14	Document of the CCP Central Committee, the State Council and the Central Military Commission	SC, CMC	2: 159 (CT) 160-161 (ET)
11 January 1967	16	Circular of the CCP Central Committee Concerning the Opposition to Economism		2: 163-164 (CT) 165-167 (ET) 8: 1967, 1574 (CT)
11 January 1967		Circular of the CCP Central Committee and the State Council Concerning the Prohibition of the Corruption of the Masses	SC	2: 169 (CT) 170 (ET)
11 January 1967		Circular of the CCP Central Committee Concerning Broadcasting Stations		2: 171 (CT) 172 (ET)

Date of Issue	CD Number	Title	Cosignatories	Source
13 January 1967	19	Some Regulations of the CCP Central Committee and the State Council Concerning the Strengthening of Public Security Work in the Great Proletarian Cultural Revolution	SC	2: 173-174 (CT) 175-177 (ET) 3: 22-23 (CT) 6: 001 B
14 January 1967		Circular of the CCP Central Committee Concerning the Prohibition of Directing the Spearhead of Struggle against the Armed Forces		2: 179-180 (CT) 181-182 (ET)
18 January 1967		Circular Telegram of the CCP Central Committee Dated January 18		2: 183 (CT) 184 (ET) 4: 62 (CT)*
19 January 1967		Document of the CCP Central Committee, the State Council and the Central Military Commission	SC, CMC	2: 185 (CT) 186 (ET)
23 January 1967		Decision of the CCP Central Committee, the State Council, the Military Commission of the Central Committee and the Cultural Revolution Group under the Central Committee Con[illegible]	SC, CMC CCRG	2: 193-194 (CT) 195-197 (ET)

		cerning the Resolute Support of People's Liberation Army for the Revolutionary Masses of the Left		
23 January 1967	29	Supplementary Circular of the CCP Central Committee Concerning the Question of Broadcasting Stations		2: 199 (CT) 200-201 (ET)
25 January 1967		Circular of the CCP Central Committee Concerning Safeguarding the Results of the Four Clean-ups Movement		2: 203 (CT) 204-205 (ET)
30 January 1967		Notice of the CCP Central Central Committee Concerning the Security Question of Confidential Secrets		25: 139 (CT)
30 January 1967		Decision of the CCP Central Committee, the State Council and the Central Military Commission Concerning the Recent Incident in Chekiang	SC, CMC	2: 219-220 (CT) 221-223 (ET)
31 January 1967		Preliminary Opinion of the CCP Central Committee Concerning How to Reform the Educational System		3: 117-122 (CT)

Date of Issue	CD Number	Title	Cosignatories	Source
February 1967		Opinions of the CCP Central Committee Concerning the Proletarian Cultural Revolution on the Streets of Cities and Towns		8: 1971, 7–13 (CT)
3 February 1967		Circular of the CCP Central Committee and the State Council Concerning the Question of Exchange of Revolutionary Experience on Foot by Revolutionary Teachers and Students and Red Guards	SC	2: 225-226 (CT) 227-229 (ET)
4 February 1967		Circular of the CCP Central Committee Concerning the Great Proletarian Cultural Revolution in Primary Schools (Draft)		2: 233-234 (CT) 235-236 (ET) 3: 122-123 (CT)
11 February 1967		Twelve Point Regulations for the Cultural Revolution in Sinkiang's Production and Construction Corps	SC, CMC	3: 147-149 (CT) 2: 255-257 (CT)* 258-261 (ET)*
12 February 1967		Circular of the CCP Central Committee Concerning the Question of Handling the Party Mem-		2: 271 (CT) 272 (ET) 8: 5-6 (CT)

	bership of Party Members		
12 February 1967	Notice of the CCP Central Committee and the State Council	SC	2: 277 (CT) 278-279 (ET)
17 February 1967	Circular of the CCP Central Committee Concerning the Question of Dealing with Work Groups in the Great Proletarian Cultural Revolution		2: 293 (CT) 294 (ET)
17 February 1967	Regulations of the CCP Central Committee and the State Council Concerning the Great Proletarian Cultural Revolution in Literary and Art Bodies	SC	2: 295-296 (CT) 297-298 (ET)
17 February 1967	Circular of the CCP Central Committee and the State Council Concerning (Urban) Educated Youths Working in Rural and Mountainous Areas Who Go Out to Exchange Revolutionary Experience, Make Petitions, or Call on People at Higher Levels	SC	2: 299-300 (CT) 301-302 (ET)
17 February 1967	Notice of the CCP Central Committee and the State Council	SC	2: 303-304 (CT) 305-306 (ET) 3: 92-93 (CT)*

Date of Issue	CD Number	Title	Cosignatories	Source
17 February 1967		Some Regulations of the CCP Central Committee and the State Council Concerning the Assurance of Security of Confidential Documents and Files	SC	2: 307-308 (CT) 309-310 (ET)
17 February 1967		Urgent Notice of the CCP Central Committee and the State Council Concerning the Need for Workers Aiding Construction in the Hinterland and Frontierland to Participate in the Great Cultural Revolution in Their Own Localities	SC	2: 311-312 (CT) 313-314 (ET)
17 February 1967		Circular Order of the CCP Central Committee Concerning Withdrawing Cultural Revolutionary Work Groups from Schools of Various Levels		3: 6 (CT)
19 February 1967		Opinion of the CCP Central Committee Concerning the Great Proletarian Cultural Revolution in Middle Schools		2: 319-320 (CT) 321-324 (ET)
19 February 1967		Circular of the CCP Central		2: 325 (CT)

		Question of Propagandizing and Reporting on the Struggle to Seize Power	
20 February 1967		Letter from the CCP Central Committee to Poor and Lower-middle Peasants and Cadres at All Levels in Rural People's Communes throughout the Country	2: 329-330 (CT) 331-333 (ET) 8: 1967, 1595-1596 (CT)
21 February 1967		Circular of the CCP Central Committee	2: 335-336 (CT) 337-338 (ET) 3: 60-61 (CT)*
7 March 1967	81	Regulations of the CCP Central Committee Concerning the Great Proletarian Cultural Revolution Currently Under Way in Universities, Colleges and Schools (Draft)	2: 341-342 (CT) 343-345 (ET)
7 March 1967	82	Circular of the CCP Central Committee Concerning the Undesirability of Seizure of Power in Rural Production Brigades and Production Teams during the Spring Farming Period	2: 347-348 (CT) 349-350 (ET)

Date of Issue	CD Number	Title	Cosignatories	Source
8 March 1967	85	Document of the CCP Central Committee Appendix I: A Directive from Chairman Mao Concerning the Great Strategic Plan for the Great Proletarian Cultural Revolution Appendix II: Understanding of the Tientsin Yenan Middle School in Realizing the Great Alliance and Reorganizing, Consolidating and Developing the Red Guards in the Whole School with the Training Class as the Foundation		2: 351-354 (CT) 355-360 (ET) 4: 84-87 (CT)*
11 March 1967		Regulations of the CCP Central Committee Concerning Creating a High Tide in Spring Farming Production		8: 1967, 1597-1598 (CT)
13 March 1967		Regulations of the CCP Central Committee Concerning Seizing Vessels		3: 96-97 (CT)
16 March 1967		Circular of the CCP Central Committee, the State Council	SC, CMC	2: 365-366 (CT) 367-368 (ET)

	tion of State Property and the Practice of Economy While Making Revolution		
18 March 1967	Letter from the Central Committee of the Chinese Communist Party to Revolutionary Workers and Staff and Revolutionary Cadres in Industrial and Mining Enterprises throughout the Country		2: 369-371 (CT) 372-375 (ET) 8: 1967, 1596 (CT)
19 March 1967	Circular of the CCP Central Committee Concerning the Suspension of the Big Exchange of Revolutionary Experience All over the Country		2: 377 (CT) 378 (ET)
20 March 1967	Some Regulations of the CCP Central Committee Concerning the Handling of Goods and Chattels Confiscated by the Red Guards in the Great Cultural Revolution Movement		2: 379 (CT) 380-381 (ET)
24 March 1967	Decision of the CCP Central Committee, the State Council, the Central Military Commission and the Central Cultural Revolution Group Concerning the Question of Tsinghai	SC, CMC, CCRG	2: 383-384 (CT) 385-387 (ET)

Date of Issue	CD Number	Title	Cosignatories	Source
27 March 1967		Decision of the CCP Central Committee Concerning the Question of Anhwei		2: 389-391 (CT) 392-395 (ET)
1 April 1967	117	Document of the CCP Central Committee Concerning Disseminating the Decision on the Anhwei Question		2: 397-398 (CT) 399-401 (ET) 3: 152-153 (CT)*
4 April 1967		Circular of the CCP Central Committee Concerning the Rehabilitation of Liu Chieh-t'ing and Others in Ipin District, Szechwan Province		2: 403-404 (CT) 405-406 (ET)
7 April 1967	123	Circular of the CCP Central Committee, the State Council, the Central Military Commission and the Central Cultural Revolution Group Concerning the Broadcasting of Comrade Lin Piao's Speech	SC, CMC, CCRG	2: 413 (CT) 414 (ET)
13 April 1967		Decision of the CCP Central Committee Concerning the Handling of the Inner Mongolia Question		2: 415-416 (CT) 417-419 (ET)

20 April 1967		Circular of the CCP Central Committee, the State Council, the Central Military Commission and the Central Cultural Revolution Group on Exchange of Revolutionary Experience by Students	SC, CMC CCRG	2: 429 (CT) 430 (ET) 3: 144 (CT)*
30 April 1967		Opinion of the CCP Central Committee Concerning the Question of Fukien		3: 154-156 (CT)
7 May 1967		Decision of the CCP Central Committee Concerning the Question of Szechwan		2: 431-433 (CT) 434-438 (ET)
11 May 1967	153	Document of the CCP Central Committee		2: 439 (CT) 440 (ET) 4: 4 (CT)*
16 May 1967		Opinion of the CCP Central Committee Concerning the Question of Chungking		2: 441-442 (CT) 443-445 (ET)
17 May 1967		Notice of the CCP Central Committee Concerning Seriously Organizing the Study and Examination of the May 16 Circular		3: 8 (CT)

Date of Issue	CD Number	Title	Cosignatories	Source
23 May 1967		Seven Directives Concerning Future Culture and Art Propaganda Works by the CCP Central Committee in Commemoration of the 25th Anniversary of the Publication of Mao Tse-tung's Talk at the Yenan Forum on Literature and Art		3: 129-130 (CT)
31 May 1967	173	Regulations of the CCP Central Committee Concerning Access to Files and Materials		8: 1971, 7-13-14 (CT)
31 May 1967	175	Document of the CCP Central Committee, the Central Military Commission, the Central Cultural Revolution Group and the Cultural Revolution Group of All-PLA	CMC, CCRG A-PLA CRG	2: 457 (CT) 458-459 (ET) 3: 164-165 (CT)*
6 June 1967		Circular Order of the CCP Central Committee, the State Council, the Central Military Commission and the Central Cultural Revolution Group Concerning the Strict Prohibition of Armed Struggle, Illegal Arrest and [illegible]	SC, CMC CCRG	2: 461-462 (CT) 463-464 (ET) 3: 37-38 (CT)*

24 June 1967	199	Circular of the CCP Central Committee		2: 465 (CT) 466-467 (ET) 4: 22-23 (CT)*
28 June 1967	200	Circular of the CCP Central Committee Concerning the Question of "Catching Renegades"		2: 469-470 (CT) 471-472 (ET)
13 July 1967	218	Circular of the CCP Central Committee Concerning the Prohibition of Instigating Peasants to Carry Out Armed Struggle in Cities		2: 473-474 (CT) 475-476 (ET) 3: 38-39 (CT)
26 July 1967		Comment of the CCP Central Committee for the Transmission of the Proclamation of the PLA Wuhan Military Region Command		2: 477 (CT) 478-479 (ET)
27 July 1967		A Letter of the CCP Central Committee, the State Council, the Central Military Commission and the Central Cultural Revolution Group to the Revolutionary Masses and Vast Commanders and Combatants of Wuhan Municipality	SC, CMC CCRG	2: 481-483 (CT) 484-488 (ET)

Date of Issue	CD Number	Title	Cosignatories	Source
14 August 1967		Decision of the CCP Central Committee Concerning the Question of Kiangsi		3: 162 (CT)
14 August 1967	251	Circular of the CCP Central Committee Concerning the Question of Criticism and Repudiation by Name in Publications		2: 495-496 (CT) 497-499 (ET)
31 August 1967		Notification of the CCP Central Committee, the State Council, the Central Military Commission and the Central Cultural Revolution Group Concerning the Seizure of State Secret Files by the "Red Combat Corps" of the Ministry of Chemical Industries	SC, CMC CCRG	2: 501-502 (CT) 503-504 (ET)
September 1967		Important Directive of the CCP Central Committee on the Question of Sinkiang		3: 149-150 (CT)
5 September 1967	288	Order of the CCP Central Committee, the State Council, the Central Military Commission	SC, CMC CCRG	2: 505-506 (CT) 507-510 (ET)

	tion Group Concerning the Prohibition of the Seizure of Arms, Equipment, and Other Military Supplies from the PLA		
9 September 1967	Circular of the General Office of the CCP Central Committee Appendix: Important Talk Given by Comrade Chiang Ch'ing on September 5 at a Conference of Representatives of Anhwei Who Have Come to Peking		2: 511-519 (CT) 520-534 (ET)
13 September 1967	Circular of the CCP Central Committee, the State Council, the Central Military Commission and the Central Cultural Revolution Group Concerning the Strict Prohibition of Seizing Materials and Commodities of the State, Raiding Godowns and Storages, to Safeguard the Properties of the State	SC, CMC CCRG	2: 535-536 (CT) 537-539 (ET)
18 September 1967	Five Instructions of the CCP Central Committee Concerning Stopping Armed Struggle in Tibet		3: 161-162 (CT)

Date of Issue	CD Number	Title	Cosignatories	Source
23 September 1967		Order of the CCP Central Committee, the State Council, the Military Affairs Committee, and the Cultural Revolution Group Concerning the Elimination of Private Radios, Broadcasting Stations and Ham Radios	SC, MAC, CCRG	3: 39–40 (CT)
23 September 1967		Circular of the CCP Central Committee, the State Council, the Military Affairs Commission, and the Cultural Revolution Group Concerning Strengthening the Work of Protecting and Maintaining Forests and Prohibiting the Destruction of Forests and Trees	SC, MAC, CCRG	3: 100–101 (CT)
23 September 1967		Urgent Circular of the CCP Central Committee, the State Council, the Military Affairs Commission, and the Cultural Revolution Group Stipulating That Students Forming Revolutionary Alliances and Personnel Visiting Peking Should Immediately Return to Original Working	SC, MAC, CCRG	3: 145–146 (CT)

28 September 1967		Circular of the CCP Central Committee Disseminating Anhwei's Enthusiastic and Thorough Implementation of K'ang Sheng's and Chiang Ch'ing's September 5 Directive		3: 154 (CT)
October 1967		Decision of the CCP Central Committee and the State Council Concerning Establishing Temporary Organs of Authority at Various Levels	SC	3: 40-41 (CT)
6 October 1967	310	Circular of the General Office of the CCP Central Committee (Note: The chung-fa number and the subject matter suggest that this circular was a Central Document rather than a document of the General Office of the CCP Central Committee)		2: 541-542 (CT) 543-544 (ET) 4: 5 (CT)*
7 October 1967	313	Circular of the CCP Central Committee Appendix: Important Directives of Chairman Mao during His Inspection Tour of the North China, Central-South and East China Regions		2: 545-549 (CT) 550-556 (ET)

Date of Issue	CD Number	Title	Cosignatories	Source
8 October 1967	312	Directive of the CCP Central Committee, the State Council, the Military Affairs Committee, and the Cultural Revolution Group Concerning the Work of Taking Over and Investigating the Files of the Enemy	SC, MAC, CCRG	8: 1971, 7–14 (CT)
8 October 1967		Urgent Circular of the CCP Central Committee, the State Council, the Central Military Commission and the Central Cultural Revolution Group Concerning the Necessity for Educated Youths and Other Personnel Assigned to Work in Rural and Mountainous Areas to Persist in Staying in the Countryside to Grasp Revolution and Promote Production	SC, CMC, CCRG	2: 557-559 (CT) 560-563 (ET)
14 October 1967		Circular of the CCP Central Committee, the State Council, the Central Military Commission and the Central Cultural Revolution Group Concerning the Resumption of Classes and	SC, CMC, CCRG	2: 565 (CT) 566-567 (ET)

		Secondary and Primary Schools		
17 October 1967		Four-Point Directive of the CCP Central Committee, the Central Military Commission, the Central Cultural Revolution Group and the All-PLA Cultural Revolution Group Concerning Propaganda Work	CMC, CCRG, A-PLA CRG	2: 571-572 (CT) 573-574 (ET)
17 October 1967		Circular of the CCP Central Committee, the State Council, the Central Military Commission and the Central Cultural Revolution Group Concerning the Forging of Revolutionary Great Alliance in Individual Systems	SC, CMC, CCRG	2: 569 (CT) 570 (ET)
26 October 1967	325	Regulations of the CCP Central Committee Concerning the Question of Forbidding Landlord, Rich-peasant, Counter-revolutionary, Bad and Rightist Elements to Avail Themselves of the Opportunity to Reverse the Sentences Passed on Them		2: 579-580 (CT) 581-582 (ET)

Date of Issue	CD Number	Title	Cosignatories	Source
5 November 1967		22 Slogans of the CCP Central Committee Commemorating the 50th Anniversary of the October Socialist Revolution		3: 10–11 (CT)
12 November 1967		Decision of the CCP Central Committee, the State Council, the Central Military Commission and the Central Cultural Revolution Group Concerning the Question of Kwangtung	SC, CMC, CCRG	2: 583–584 (CT) 585–588 (ET)
13 November 1967	354	Document of the CCP Central Committee Appendix: Talk of Comrade Chiang Ch'ing	CCRG	2: 589–594 (CT) 595–602 (ET)
18 November 1967		Decision of the CCP Central Committee, the State Council, the Central Military Commission and the Central Cultural Revolution Group Concerning the Question of Kwangsi	SC, CMC, CCRG	2: 603–604 (CT) 605–607 (ET)
27 November 1967	358	Notification of the CCP Central Committee and the Central Cultural Revolution Group Concern-	CCRG	2: 609–613 (CT) 614–621 (ET)

		ing the Inquiry of Opinions on the Convening of the "Ninth Congress"		
27 November 1967		Circular Order of the CCP Central Committee and the Cultural Revolution Group Concerning Prohibiting the Reprinting of Unpublished Photographs and Works of Mao Which Have Not Been Investigated and Approved by the Party Center	CCRG	3: 41-42 (CT)
2 December 1967	367	Circular of the CCP Central Committee, the State Council, the Central Military Commission and the Central Cultural Revolution Group Concerning the Correct Handling of Old Rebels Who Have Committed Mistakes	SC, CMC, CCRG	2: 623-624 (CT) 625-626 (ET)
2 December 1967		Circular Order of the CCP Central Committee, the State Council, the Military Affairs Committee, and the Cultural Revolution Group Concerning Protecting the Security of Railway Transportation and Goods	SC, MAC, CCRG	3: 103-104 (CT)

Date of Issue	CD Number	Title	Cosignatories	Source
4 December 1967		Directive of the CCP Central Committee Concerning the Great Cultural Revolution in the Countryside in This Winter and Next Spring		2: 627-629 (CT) 630-633 (ET) 3: 105-106 (CT)*
7 December 1967	373	Circular of the CCP Central Committee, the State Council, the Central Military Commission and the Central Cultural Revolution Group Concerning the Serious Study and Firm Implementation of "Chairman Mao's Comment on the Educational Revolution"	SC, CMC, CCRG	2: 635-636 (CT) 637-638 (ET) 4: 74-75 (CT)--mistakenly dates this CD as 7 February 1967
14 December 1967		Comment of the CCP Central Committee, the State Council, the Military Affairs Committee, and the Cultural Revolution Group Concerning the Circular Regarding the Party Committee in the Shantung Military Region	SC, MAC CCRG	4: 100-101 (CT)
16 December 1967	384	The CCP Central Committee Approves the Addition of Five Members to the Hunan Provin-		2: 639 (CT) 640 (ET)

		Preparatory Group		
20 December 1967		CCP Central Committee Document on Opinions and Problems Concerning Rectifying, Restoring, and Reconstructing the Party Organization		4: 6-9 (CT) 3: 15-17 (PCT)
22 December 1967	396	Comment of the CCP Central Committee and the Central Cultural Revolution Group Concerning the Examinations of Comrades P'an Fu-sheng and Wang Chia-tao	CCRG	2: 641-642 (CT) 643-644 (ET) 4: 101-103 (CT)
15 January 1968	9	Regulations of the CCP Central Committee, the State Council, the Military Affairs Committee, and the Cultural Revolution Group Concerning the Question of External Investigations	SC, MAC, CCRG	8: 1971, 7-14-15 (CT)
18 January 1968		Circular of the CCP Central Committee, the State Council, the Military Affairs Committee and the Cultural Revolution Group Concerning Intensifying the Work of Striking at Counter-revolutionary Economism and Speculative Activities	SC, MAC, CCRG	3: 109-112 (CT)

Date of Issue	CD Number	Title	Cosignatories	Source
5 February 1968		Comment of the CCP Central Committee Concerning the Distribution of the Report of the Heilungkiang Provincial Revolutionary Committee on the Situation in the Work of Digging Out Traitors Appendix: Report of the Heilungkiang Provincial Revolutionary Committee on the Situation of Digging Out Traitors Distributed by the CCP Central Committee		8: 1971, 7–16–17 (CT)
5 February 1968		Directive of the CCP Central Committee, the State Council, the Military Affairs Committee, and the Cultural Revolution Group Concerning Doing Further Good Work in the Files to Unearth the Enemy	SC, MAC, CCRG	8: 1971, 7–15–16 (CT)
20 February 1968		Comment of the CCP Central Committee, the State Council, the Military Affairs Committee, and the Cultural Revolution Group Concerning the Establishment of the Kwangtung Provincial [illegible]	SC, MAC, CCRG	4: 102–104 (CT)

22 March 1968		Order of the CCP Central Committee, the State Council, the Central Military Affairs Committee, and the Central Cultural Revolution Group Concerning the Dismissals of Yang Ch'eng-wu, Yu Li-chin and Fu Sung-pi from Office	SC, MAC, CCRG	6: 001 C (CT)
April 1968	61	Comment of the CCP Central Committee, the State Council, the Military Affairs Committee, and the Cultural Revolution Group Concerning the Establishment of the Anhwei Provincial Revolutionary Committee	SC, MAC, CCRG	4: 104-106 (CT) 6: 001 C (CT)
20 April 1968		Several Directives of the CCP Central Committee, the State Council and the Central Military Commission on the Cotton Cloth Supply for 1968	SC, CMC	1: 837-838 (ET) 4: 69 (CT)
20 May 1968		Comment of the CCP Central Committee, the State Council, the Military Affairs Committee, and the Cultural Revolution Group Concerning the Resolutions of the National Conference on Railway Communications	SC, MAC, CCRG	4: 71 (CT)

Date of Issue	CD Number	Title	Cosignatories	Source
25 May 1968		Circular of the CCP Central Committee and the Cultural Revolution Group Concerning the Dissemination of Chairman Mao's Comment on the Experience of the Military Control Committee of the Peking Hsinhua Printing Company in Mobilizing the Masses to Struggle against the Enemy Appendix: Experience of the Military Control Committee	CCRG	4: 26-32 (CT)
28 May 1968	75	Comment of the CCP Central Committee, the State Council, the Military Affairs Committee, and the Cultural Revolution Group on the Establishment of the Szechwan Provincial Revolutionary Committee	SC, MAC, CCRG	3: 159-160 (CT)
10 June 1968		Various Directives of the CCP Central Committee, the State Council, the Military Affairs Committee, and the Cultural Revolution Group Concerning Troops Which Support the Left Entering Various Major Military	SC, MAC, CCRG	3: 75-78 (CT)

		Regions and Provincial Military Districts		
13 June 1968		Cable of the CCP Central Committee, the State Council, the Central Military Affairs Committee and the Central Cultural Revolutionary Group to the Ministry of Railways	SC, MAC, CCRG	6: 001C (CT)
15 June 1968	94	Circular of the CCP Central Committee, the State Council, the Military Affairs Committee, and the Cultural Revolution Group Concerning the Distribution of Graduates of Specialized Secondary Schools, Technical Schools, and Half-work Half-study Schools in 1967	SC, MAC, CCRG	4: 79-80 (CT)
3 July 1968		Bulletin of the CCP Central Committee, the State Council, the Military Affairs Committee, and the Cultural Revolution Group Concerning the Question of Kwangsi	SC, MAC, CCRG	4: 111-113 (CT)

Date of Issue	CD Number	Title	Cosignatories	Source
24 July 1968		Bulletin of the CCP Central Committee, the State Council, the Military Affairs Committee, and the Cultural Revolution Group Concerning the Question of Shensi	SC, MAC, CCRG	4: 113-115 (CT)
18 October 1968		A Report by the CCP Central Committee's Special Panel on Renegade, Traitor, and Scab Liu Shao-ch'i's Crimes		1: 243-250 (ET) 4: 9-14 (CT) 8: 1969, 7-7-9 (CT)
31 October 1968		Decision of the Enlarged 12th Plenary Session of the CCP 8th Central Committee on the "Constitution of the CCP" (Draft)		1: 235-241 (ET) 7: 1968, #24, 101-104 (M) 8: 1969, 7-4-6 (CT)
31 October 1968		Communique of the Enlarged 12th Plenary Session of the 8th Central Committee of the CCP		1: 227-234 (ET) 6: 001C (CT) 10: 1968, #5, 27-32 (CT)
8 February 1969		Circular of the CCP Central Committee Concerning Winter Vacation in Schools		4: 80 (CT)
11 February 1969		The CCP Central Committee [illegible]	CCRG	4: 115-116 (CT)

		Group on Problems to Which One Should Pay Attention in Conducting the Cultural Revolution in the Tibet Region	
28 April 1969		Communique of the First Plenary Session of the Ninth Central Committee of the CCP	16: 4/30/69, #18, 48-49 (ET)
23 July 1969		The CCP Central Committee's "Bulletin of July 23"	4: 395-397 (CT)
28 August 1969	55	Order of the CCP Central Committee Concerning Protecting the Frontier	7: 1969, #36, 98-99 (CT)
31 January 1970	2	Circular of the CCP Central Committee Concerning the Prevention and Treatment of Schistosomiasis in 13 Southern Provinces, Municipalities and Districts Appendix: Report on the Situation	8: 1974, 7–2-6 (CT)
19 May 1970	31	Circular of the CCP Central Committee Concerning the Dissemination of the Investigative Report on Tapeworm and Hookworm Diseases Issued by the Leading Group of the Committee	8: 1974, 7–7-9 (CT)

Date of Issue	CD Number	Title	Cosignatories	Source
		on the Prevention and Treatment of Schistosomiasis and the Military Control Committee of the Ministry of Public Health		
27 June 1970	49	Circular of the CCP Central Committee Concerning the Report on the Progress in the Work of Schistosomiasis-prevention in 13 Southern Provinces, Municipalities and Districts Appendices: Reports on the Progress		8: 1974, 7–9–14 (CT)
6 September 1970		Communique of the Second Plenary Session of the Ninth Central Committee of the CCP		13: 9/10/70 (CT) 16: #37, 1970, 5–7 (ET)
12 September 1970	56	Notice of the CCP Central Committee Concerning a Cover Letter for Distribution of the Draft Constitution for Discussion Appendix: Text of the Draft Constitution		5: 106–108 (ET)
14 September 1971	57	Chairman Mao's Open Letter to the the Whole Party		5: 67–68 (PET)

18 September 1971	60	Communique of the CCP Central Committee Concerning Lin Piao's "September 12" Anti-party Incident	5: 69-70 (PET)
1971	61	Communique of the CCP Central Committee Concerning the Lin-ch'en Anti-party Clique	5: 71-73 (PET)
1971	62	Decision of the CCP Central Committee Concerning the Lin-ch'en Anti-party Clique	5: 74-75 (PET)
November 1971	64	Notice of the CCP Central Committee Concerning the Discarding of the "Four Good" and "Five Good" Movements and the Turning In to Higher Authorities of the Epitaphs and Portraits of Lin Piao	5: 76-77 (PET)
1971	68	(Title and date unknown: on the Lin Piao affair)	11: 1974, #3, 7, 12-13, 16-19, 26-27 (M)
1971	77	(Title and date unknown: on the Lin Piao affair)	11: 1974, #3, 7, 12-13, 16-19, 26-27 (M)
26 December 1971	82	Directive of the CCP Central Committee Concerning the Question of Distribution in Rural People's Communes	8: 1973, 7-3-4 (CT)

Date of Issue	CD Number	Title	Cosignatories	Source
Late 1971 (?)		"On strengthening the leadership of the Party and circulating the minutes of the Canton Military Region conference"		11: 1974, #3, 29-30 (M)
Early January 1972	3	(Title unknown--stipulates the scope for circulation of subsequent Central Documents pertaining to the Lin Piao affair)		5: 56, 79 (M)
13 January 1972	4	Notice of the CCP Central Committee Concerning the Struggle to Smash the Lin-Ch'en Anti-party Clique's Counterrevolutionary Coup (Materials Part II)		5: 78-79, 80-95 (ET) 8: 1972, 6-8 (CT)*
17 March 1972	12	Notice of the CCP Central Committee on Summary of Chairman Mao's Talks to Responsible Local Comrades during His Tour of Inspection		5: 55-56, 57-66 (ET) 8: 1973, 7-5-8 (CT)*
2 July 1972	24	Notice of the CCP Central Committee Concerning the Struggle to Smash the Counterrevolutionary Coup d'etat of the Lin Piao Anti-party Clique (Materials Part III)		5: 96-105 (ET) 8: 1973, 7-8-10 (CT)*

September 1972	25	"Criticisms of Lin Piao's works and speeches" in Mao Tse-tung's private letter to Chiang Ch'ing dated July 8, 1966	5: 118-121 (ET) 8: 1973, 7–2 (CT)
8 September 1973	34	Notice of the CCP Central Committee Concerning Report on the Investigation of the Counter-revolutionary Crimes of the Lin Piao Anti-party Clique	5: 110-117 (ET) 8: 1974, 7–14-17 (CT)*
18 January 1974	1	Circular of the CCP Central Committee Concerning the Dissemination of the First Group of Materials on "Lin Piao and the Ways of Confucius and Mencius" Compiled by Peking and Tsinghua Universities Appendix	8: 1975, 6–12-20 (CT)
22 January 1974	2	Circular of the CCP Central Committee Concerning the Distribution of Supplementary Materials on Studying and Discussing <u>Chung-fa</u> (1974) #1	8: 1974, 7–17 (CT)
25 January 1974	3	Document of the CCP Central Committee Concerning the Dissemination of the Report of the	8: 1974, 7–17-19 (CT)

Date of Issue	CD Number	Title	Cosignatories	Source
		Nanking Military District CCP Committee to the Party Center and the Letters of the 20th Army Committee and the Anti-chemical Warfare Company to Comrade Chiang Ch'ing Appendix I: Report of the Nanking Military District CCP Committee on Learning from Comrade Chiang Ch'ing's Letter to the Anti-chemical Warfare Company Appendix II: Letter of the PLA 20th Army Committee to Comrade Chiang Ch'ing Appendix III: Letter of the 2081 Troop Anti-chemical Warfare Company to Comrade Chiang Ch'ing		
1974	13	(Title unknown--prohibits cross-area and cross-trade exchange of experiences, establishing mountain strongholds and fighting civil wars)		12: 1975, #1, 103 (M)
1 July 1974	21	Circular of the CCP Central Committee Concerning Grasping		8: 1975, 6–20 (CT) 12: 1975, #1, 101-104 (ET)

		Revolution and Promoting Production	
October 1974	26	(Title unknown--emergency measures on the economy)	8: 1975, 2–88 (M)
1975 (probably spring)		Document of the CCP Central Committee on speeding up development of iron and steel industry	9: 4/2/77, 4/21/77 (M) 13: 7/7/77 (M) 14: 4/4/77, E5; 4/26/77, E8; 4/14/77, E18; 7/8/77, E6 (M) 15: 3/23/77 (M)
1975 (probably March)		Decision of the CCP Central Committee on strengthening railway service	9: 2/15/77, 2/20/77, 3/9/77 4/17/77 (M) 13: 3/12/77, 1; 7/7/77 (M) 14: 2/18/77, E1; 2/22/77, E1; 3/10/77, E3; 4/18/77, E7; 7/8/77, E6 (M)
May 1975		(Title unknown--on naval construction)	9: 3/14/77 (M) 14: 3/16/77 (M)
July 1975		(Title unknown--on military affairs	14: 3/23/77, E15-16 (M) 17: 3/15/77 (M)
3 February 1976	1	(Title unknown--appoints Hua Kuo-feng as acting premier of the State Council)	13: 12/13/76, 6/3/77 (M) 14: 6/6/77, E16 (M) 19: 3/15/77, 1; 3/22/77, 6 (M)

Date of Issue	CD Number	Title	Cosignatories	Source
Spring 1976		(Title unknown--on keeping the army stable)	MAC	16: 3/4/77, #10, 11 (M)
7 April 1976		Resolution of the CPC Central Committee on Appointing Comrade Hua Kuo-feng First Vice-Chairman of the CPC Central Committee and Premier of State Council		16: 4/9/76, #15, 3 (ET)
7 April 1976		Resolution of the CPC Central Committee on Dismissing Teng Hsiao-p'ing from All Posts Both Inside and Outside Party		16: 4/9/76, #15, 3 (ET)
1976	16	(Title unknown--on the "Gang of Four")		14: 2/10/77, E13 (M) 19: 2/7/77, (M)
18 October 1976	18	(Title unknown--directive on handling pictures of the "Gang of Four")		20: 11/10/76 (PCT)
Late October 1976		(Title unknown--circular on convening the 3rd Plenum of the 10th Central Committee)		14: 4/9/77, E1 (M) 20: 3/30/77 (M)

1976 (probably November)		(Title unknown--notice on handling the Paoting problem)	9: 2/27/77 (M) 14: 2/28/77, E19-20 (M)
Early November 1976	19	Emergency Circular on Freezing the Accounts of Various Units	14: 2/10/77, E12-13 (M) 19: 2/7/77 (M) 20: 11/17/76 (PCT)
Late 1976	21	"On Teng Hsiao-p'ing"	14: 3/14/77, E5 (M) 19: 3/15/77 (CT) 21: 3/6/77 (M)
December 1976		(Title unknown--circular on convening the 3rd Plenum of the 10th Central Committee)	14: 4/9/77, E1 (M) 20: 3/30/77 (M)
10 December 1976	24	Criminal Evidence of the Wang Hung-wen, Chang Ch'un-ch'iao, Chiang Ching, Yao Wen-yuan Anti-party Clique (1st Materials)	7: 1977, 11:7, 103-160 (PCT) 8: 1977 (CT) 12: 1977, #9, 80-105 (ET) 12: 1977, #10, 79-112 (ET) 12: 1977, #11, 85-112 (ET)
1977 (?)		(Title unknown--instructions on railway work)	9: 3/16/77 (M) 14: 3/17/77, E4 (M)
1977 (?)		(Title unknown--instructions concerning Yunnan)	22: 2/27/77 (M) 14: 3/1/77, J2-3 (M)
January 1977		(Title unknown--on implementing tasks specified by second Tachai Conference and post-	14: 4/6/77, E1 (M) 20: 3/30/77 (M)

Date of Issue	CD Number	Title	Cosignatories	Source
		poning 3rd Plenum of 10th Central Committee)		
5 January 1977		(Title unknown--document on rehabilitation of Teng Hsiao p'ing after he adequately confesses his error)		23: 3/17/77 (M) 14: 3/17/77, E1-2 (M)
Early 1977	5	(Title unknown--on investigating certain political rumors)		14: 3/30/77, N1 (M) 19: 3/29/77 (M)
Early 1977		(Title unknown--absolves Teng Hsiao-p'ing of culpability for the April 1976 Tienanmen Incident)		23: 3/17/77 (M) 14: 3/17/77, E1-2 (M)
March 1977		(Title unknown--second set of materials generated by the investigation of the "Gang of Four")		19: 4/2/77 (M)
7 April 1977		"Decision of the Central Committee of the Communist Party of China on studying volume 5 of the 'Selected Works of Mao Tse-tung'"		9: 4/14/77 (ET) 14: 4/14/77, E3-5 (ET)

3 May 1977	15	(Title unknown--contains texts of letters written by Teng Hsiao-p'ing to Hua Kuo-feng on 10 October 1976 and 10 April 1977 respectively)	19: 5/27/77, 1 (PCT)
Early August 1977		(Title unknown--on policy and tasks for industry and communications during last five months of 1977)	14: 8/17/77, H1-3 (M) 24: 8/14/77 (M)
18 September 1977		Circular on Holding National Science Conference	14: 9/22/77, E1-3 (PET) 9: 9/22/77 (PET) 16: 9/30/77, #40, 6-11 (ET)
5 October 1977		Decision on Doing a Good Job of Running Party Schools at Various Levels	9: 10/9/77 (CT) 14: 10/11/77, E1-5 (ET)
Early fall 1977		(Title unknown--on discussing the possibility of re-establishing the post of chairman of the PRC)	26: 12/10/77, 2 (M)

MICHIGAN PAPERS IN CHINESE STUDIES

No. 2. The Cultural Revolution: 1967 in Review, four essays by Michel Oksenberg, Carl Riskin, Robert Scalapino, and Ezra Vogel.

No. 3. Two Studies in Chinese Literature, by Li Chi and Dale Johnson.

No. 4. Early Communist China: Two Studies, by Ronald Suleski and Daniel Bays.

No. 5. The Chinese Economy, ca. 1870-1911, by Albert Feuerwerker.

No. 6. Chinese Paintings in Chinese Publications, 1956-1968: An Annotated Bibliography and an Index to the Paintings, by E. J. Laing.

No. 7. The Treaty Ports and China's Modernization: What Went Wrong? by Rhoads Murphey.

No. 8. Two Twelfth Century Texts on Chinese Painting, by Robert J. Maeda.

No. 9. The Economy of Communist China, 1949-1969, by Chu-yuan Cheng.

No. 10. Educated Youth and the Cultural Revolution in China, by Martin Singer.

No. 11. Premodern China: A Bibliographical Introduction, by Chun-shu Chang.

No. 12. Two Studies on Ming History, by Charles O. Hucker.

No. 13. Nineteenth Century China: Five Imperialist Perspectives, selected by Dilip Basu, edited by Rhoads Murphey.

No. 14. Modern China, 1840-1972: An Introduction to Sources and Research Aids, by Andrew J. Nathan.

No. 15. Women in China: Studies in Social Change and Feminism, edited by Marilyn B. Young.

No. 16. An Annotated Bibliography of Chinese Painting Catalogues and Related Texts, by Hin-cheung Lovell.

No. 17. China's Allocation of Fixed Capital Investment, 1952-1957, by Chu-yuan Cheng.

No. 18. Health, Conflict, and the Chinese Political System, by David M. Lampton.

No. 19. Chinese and Japanese Music-Dramas, edited by J. I. Crump and William P. Malm.

No. 21. Rebellion in Nineteenth-Century China, by Albert Feuerwerker.

No. 22. Between Two Plenums: China's Intraleadership Conflict, 1959-1962, by Ellis Joffe.

No. 23. "Proletarian Hegemony" in the Chinese Revolution and the Canton Commune of 1927, by S. Bernard Thomas.

No. 24. Chinese Communist Materials at the Bureau of Investigation Archives, Taiwan, by Peter Donovan, Carl E. Dorris, and Lawrence R. Sullivan.

No. 25. Shanghai Old-Style Banks (Ch'ien-chuang), 1800-1935, by Andrea Lee McElderry.

No. 26. The Sian Incident: A Pivotal Point in Modern Chinese History, by Tien-wei Wu.

No. 27. State and Society in Eighteenth-Century China: The Ch'ing Empire in Its Glory, by Albert Feuerwerker.

No. 28. Intellectual Ferment for Political Reforms in Taiwan, 1971-1973, by Mab Huang.

No. 29. The Foreign Establishment in China in the Early Twentieth Century, by Albert Feuerwerker.

No. 30. A Translation of Lao Tzu's "Tao Te Ching" and Wang Pi's "Commentary," by Paul J. Lin.

No. 31. Economic Trends in the Republic of China, 1912-1949, by Albert Feuerwerker.

No. 32. Chang Ch'un-ch'iao and Shanghai's January Revolution, by Andrew G. Walder.

No. 33. Central Documents and Politburo Politics in China, by Kenneth Lieberthal.

MICHIGAN ABSTRACTS OF CHINESE AND JAPANESE WORKS ON CHINESE HISTORY

No. 1. The Ming Tribute Grain System, by Hoshi Ayao, translated by Mark Elvin.

No. 2. Commerce and Society in Sung China, by Shiba Yoshinobu, translated by Mark Elvin.

No. 3. Transport in Transition: The Evolution of Traditional Shipping in China, translations by Andrew Watson.

No. 4. Japanese Perspectives on China's Early Modernization: A Bibliographical Survey, by K. H. Kim.

No. 5. The Silk Industry in Ch'ing China, by Shih Min-hsiung, translated by E-tu Zen Sun.

NONSERIES PUBLICATION

Index to the "Chan-kuo Ts'e," by Sharon Fidler and J. I. Crump. A companion volume to the Chan-kuo Ts'e, translated by J. I. Crump (Oxford: Clarendon Press, 1970).

Michigan Papers and Abstracts available from:

Center for Chinese Studies
The University of Michigan
Lane Hall (Publications)
Ann Arbor, MI 48109 USA

Prepaid Orders Only
write for complete price listing

Printed and bound by CPI Group (UK) Ltd, Croydon, CR0 4YY

13/04/2025

14656507-0003